Collins

# Cambridge IGCSE®

# Accounting

## WORKBOOK

### Also for Cambridge O Level

David Horner, Leanna Oliver

William Collins' dream of knowledge for all began with the publication of his first book in 1819.

A self-educated mill worker, he not only enriched millions of lives, but also founded a flourishing publishing house. Today, staying true to this spirit, Collins books are packed with inspiration, innovation and practical expertise. They place you at the centre of a world of possibility and give you exactly what you need to explore it.

Collins. Freedom to teach.

Published by Collins

An imprint of HarperCollins*Publishers*
The News Building
1 London Bridge Street
London
SE1 9GF

HarperCollins*Publishers* Macken House
39/40 Mayor Street Upper
Dublin 1
DO1 C9W8
Ireland

This book contains FSC™ certified paper and other controlled sources to ensure responsible forest management.

For more information visit: www.harpercollins.co.uk/green

The publishers gratefully acknowledge the permission granted to reproduce the copyright material in this book. Every effort has been made to trace copyright holders and to obtain their permission for the use of copyright material. The publishers will gladly receive any information enabling them to rectify any error or omission at the first opportunity.

Browse the complete Collins catalogue at
**www.collins.co.uk**

British Library Cataloguing in Publication Data

A catalogue record for this publication is available from the British Library.

Authors: David Horner, Leanna Oliver
Development editor: Penny Nicholson
Commissioning editor: Lucy Cooper
Project manager: Amanda Harman
In-house editors: Alexander Rutherford, Letitia Luff
Copyeditor: Patricia Hewson
Proofreader: Piers Maddox
Illustrator: Jouve India
Cover designers: Kevin Robbins and Gordon MacGilp
Cover illustrator: Maria Herbert-Liew
Internal designer/typesetter: Jouve India
Production controller: Tina Paul
Printed and bound by: Ashford Colour Ltd
All exam-style questions and sample answers in this title were written by the authors. In examinations, the way marks are awarded may be different.

® IGCSE is a registered trademark.

# Contents

# Introduction

Welcome to **Collins Cambridge IGCSE Accounting Workbook** which has been carefully designed and written to give you extra practice to help you succeed in the *Cambridge IGCSE Accounting* and *Cambridge O level Accounting* courses.

## How to use this book

The Student's Book covers all the content for the *Cambridge IGCSE Accounting* and *Cambridge O level Accounting* syllabuses. This Workbook supports the Student's Book and follows the same structure to allow easy cross-referencing between the books. The focus of the Workbook is to provide differentiated practice of the calculations and the techniques for preparing accounting documents required by the syllabus.

Each unit in the Workbook begins with a **Check your progress** table. This is designed to be used in conjunction with the Check your progress feature included at the end of each unit in the Student's Book. The table lists the objectives of the unit so that you can consider each in turn and reflect on your progress and understanding. Tick the column which best describes your progress after completing the work in the Student's Book, using this key:

 I struggle with this.

 I can do this reasonably well.

 I can do this with confidence.

- If you tick mostly column 1, start with the **Support** questions to support your learning.
- If you tick mostly columns 2 or 3, focus on the **Practice** questions to consolidate your learning and then move on to the **Stretch** questions.

In addition, you may also find it useful to refer to:

- the **glossary** in the Student's Book to help you learn the definitions of key terms associated with accounting.
- the **key knowledge** boxes in the Student's Book which summarise key theoretical aspects of accounting with which you need to be familiar to maximise your understanding.

At the end of each unit in the Workbook, there is a short **Unit review** with multiple-choice questions to provide an additional check of your progress with the material in the unit.

At the end of each chapter in the Workbook, there is a **Chapter review**. Like the Chapter review in the Student's Book, this allows you to practise what you have learned in the chapter with multiple-choice questions designed to help you review your progress and prepare for examination.

We hope you find this Workbook useful and wish you success in your study of accounting.

# 1 The fundamentals of accounting

## 1.1 The purpose of accounting

### Check your progress

| Read the unit objectives below. Tick the column that best describes your progress in each. | ▲ | ▲▲ | ▲▲▲ |
|---|---|---|---|
| understand and explain the difference between book-keeping and accounting | | | |
| state the purposes of measuring business profit and loss | | | |
| explain the role of accounting in providing information for monitoring progress and decision-making. | | | |

### Support

1   Which of the following are common business objectives?

    **(a)** Profit maximisation      **(b)** Income statement      **(c)** Book-keeping

    **(d)** Survival      **(e)** Market share      **(f)** Statement of financial position

### Practice

2   The total income for a business for 2018 is $78 000. For the same period, total expenses are $32 000. Calculate the profit for 2018.

### Stretch

3   State two reasons why profit may not be viewed as important by a business owner.

### Unit review

1   Which of the following is not a reason why the measurement of profit is important for a business?

    **A** To calculate tax payable

    **B** To encourage investors into the business

    **C** To obtain credit from suppliers

    **D** To help decide whether to allow credit to customers

2   Which of the following is not normally considered to be part of management accounting?

    **A** Setting targets          **C** Analysing results

    **B** Producing budgets     **D** Entering transactions in accounts

# 1.2 The accounting equation

## Check your progress

| Read the unit objectives below. Tick the column that best describes your progress in each. | ▲ | ▲▲ | ▲▲ |
|---|---|---|---|
| explain the meaning of assets, liabilities and owner's equity | | | |
| explain and apply the accounting equation. | | | |

## Support

1   Total assets are $89000 and total liabilities are $23500. Calculate the value of the owner's equity.

2   Liabilities total $11200 and the owner's equity is valued at $47500. Calculate the value of the business assets.

3   Use the following information to calculate the value of the owner's equity.

Equipment   $560                  Bank   $1120                  Bank loan   $260

## Practice

4   A business has the following assets and liabilities at the year end. Calculate the value of the owner's equity for the business.

|  | $ |
|---|---|
| Bank | 1890 |
| Machinery | 15700 |
| Vehicle | 4310 |
| Inventory | 600 |
| Loan | 5000 |
| Amounts owing to credit suppliers | 1110 |

5   Use the following information to prepare a statement of financial position.

|  | $ |
|---|---|
| Business van | 11900 |
| Owner's equity | 12000 |
| Equipment | 4155 |
| Trade receivables | 990 |
| Trade payables | 2310 |
| Bank | 1109 |
| Inventory | 656 |
| Bank loan | 4500 |

## Stretch

**6** Explain how an owner withdrawing cash from a business for personal use would affect the statement of financial position.

**7** Raj has provided the following statement of financial position.

Prepare an updated statement of financial position after the following transactions.

| Assets | $ | Liabilities and owner's equity | $ |
|---|---|---|---|
| Machinery | 24000 | Owner's equity | 25000 |
| Car | 7500 | Amount owing to friend | 10000 |
| Inventory | 2140 | Trade payables | 920 |
| Trade receivables | 1390 | | |
| Bank | 890 | | |
| | 35920 | | 35920 |

Transaction 1: A bank loan of $10000 is obtained to buy machinery for $8000.

Transaction 2: The amount owing to the friend is settled in return for the rest of the amount borrowed from the bank, the car, and the remaining balance is settled by giving the friend inventory of the value needed to clear the debt to the friend.

## Unit review

**1** Which of the following is not a liability?

    **A** Trade payables                    **C** Bank loan

    **B** Trade receivables              **D** Mortgage

**2** Use the following information to calculate the value of the owner's equity: Equipment $454, Inventory $131, Cash $654, Trade payables $646.

    **A** $1239             **B** $646                 **C** $876                 **D** $593

**3** Which of the following is correct?

| | Assets $ | Liabilities $ | Owner's equity $ |
|---|---|---|---|
| A | 3123 | 1416 | 1708 |
| B | 4341 | 647 | 3696 |
| C | 5435 | 2311 | 3124 |
| D | 6472 | 4898 | 1572 |

**4** Which of the following is incorrect?

| | Assets $ | Liabilities $ | Owner's equity $ |
|---|---|---|---|
| A | 989 | 120 | 769 |
| B | 432 | 111 | 321 |
| C | 878 | 245 | 633 |
| D | 1131 | 341 | 790 |

# Chapter 1 review

1  Which of the following is a possible objective of a business?

   **A** Book-keeping
   **B** Financial statements
   **C** Payment of tax
   **D** Breaking even

2  A business sells 750 units of output at $11.40 each and total expenses are $5488. Calculate the profit of the business.

   **A** $8550
   **B** $5488
   **C** $3062
   **D** $11 400

3  Which of the following is not a likely use of profits in a business?

   **A** Payment of dividends
   **B** Withdrawals by owner
   **C** Expansion of business
   **D** Paying customers

4  A new small business is operating in a period of economic uncertainty. What is its most likely objective?

   **A** Survival
   **B** Profit maximisation
   **C** Market share growth
   **D** Market dominance

5  Which of the following is not an asset?

   **A** Buildings
   **B** Amounts owing from customers
   **C** Mortgage on property
   **D** Inventory

6  Which of the following is an asset?

   **A** Trade receivables
   **B** Owner's equity
   **C** Money owing to suppliers
   **D** Bank loan

7  Which of the following is not correct?

|   | Assets ($) | Liabilities ($) | Owner's equity ($) |
|---|---|---|---|
| A | 6541 | 4311 | 2230 |
| B | 8745 | 3132 | 5613 |
| C | 6551 | 1312 | 4239 |
| D | 8966 | 6464 | 2502 |

8  Which of the following is correct?

|   | Assets ($) | Liabilities ($) | Owner's equity ($) |
|---|---|---|---|
| A | 16700 | 8755 | 6945 |
| B | 24510 | 8900 | 15610 |
| C | 31340 | 13755 | 17885 |
| D | 54535 | 21011 | 33424 |

**9** Use the following information to calculate the value of the owner's equity. [10]

|  | $ |
|---|---|
| Buildings | 165000 |
| Machinery | 18900 |
| Bank loan | 50000 |
| Inventory | 5542 |
| Trade payables | 8756 |
| Trade receivables | 9991 |
| Bank balance | 1010 |
| Equipment | 5000 |
| Van | 7600 |

**10** Use the following information for Bonika to prepare a statement of financial position as at 31 December 2018. The owner's equity is missing and is assumed to be the amount needed to balance the statement. [11]

|  | $ |
|---|---|
| Premises | 250000 |
| Equipment | 34000 |
| Mortgage on premises | 175000 |
| Inventory | 550 |
| Trade payables | 141 |
| Trade receivables | 544 |
| Bank balance | 2400 |
| Motor vehicle | 11000 |
| Cash in till | 43 |

**11**

| Statement of financial position | | | |
|---|---|---|---|
|  | $ |  | $ |
| Premises | 120000 | Owner's equity | 81430 |
| Equipment | 12500 | Bank loan | 60000 |
| Inventory | 5690 | Trade payables | 4430 |
| Trade receivables | 6780 |  |  |
| Bank balance | 890 |  |  |
|  | 145860 |  | 145860 |

Keletso has provided the following statement of financial position.

Prepare an updated statement of financial position after these additional transactions: [6]

Transaction 1: Inventory valued at $1290 purchased on credit.

Transaction 2: Owner withdraws $50 from the bank account for personal use.

# 2 Sources and recording of data

## 2.1 The double entry system of book-keeping

### Check your progress

| Read the unit objectives below. Tick the column that best describes your progress in each. | ▲ | ▲▲ | ▲▲ |
|---|---|---|---|
| outline the double entry system of book-keeping | | | |
| process accounting data using the double entry system | | | |
| prepare ledger accounts | | | |
| post transactions to the ledger accounts | | | |
| balance ledger accounts as required and make transfers to financial statements | | | |
| interpret ledger accounts and their balances | | | |
| recognise the division of the ledger into the sales ledger, the purchases ledger and the nominal (general ledger). | | | |

### Support

1    State whether the following are true or false.

    **(a)**  Increasing an asset's balance requires a debit entry in the asset account.

    **(b)**  Reducing the size of an amount owing requires a credit entry in the liability account.

    **(c)**  Borrowing money affects both assets and owner's equity.

    **(d)**  Paying back a loan reduces assets and liabilities.

    **(e)**  Selling an asset for cash will leave the total value of assets unchanged.

### Practice

2    Prepare the double entry accounts to record the transactions for August 2018 for Ibrahim's business.

| | |
|---|---|
| 1 August | Ibrahim places $500 of his own money into the business cash till. |
| 4 August | Ibrahim places $3000 of his own money into the business bank account. |
| 7 August | Machinery is bought for $500 with payment made by cheque. |
| 15 August | Equipment is bought on credit for $750 from Bracha. |
| 19 August | A motor car is bought on credit for $2400 from Chidike. |
| 22 August | A cheque is sent to Bracha for $750. |

**3** Prepare the double entry accounts to record the transactions for S Sial's first month of business operations.

| | |
|---|---|
| 6 October | $19000 of owner's money is placed into business bank account. |
| 10 October | Premises are bought for $15000, payment is made by cheque. |
| 15 October | $1000 from bank is paid into cash till. |
| 18 October | Fixtures and fittings are purchased for $3500 on credit from Citra. |
| 21 October | Office equipment is bought for $500 cash. |
| 24 October | Fixtures and fittings worth $750 are sold for $750 on credit to Dalitso. |

**4** Prepare the double entry accounts to record the following transactions. (You can assume that although there is no debit entry in the cash account there is money there.)

| | |
|---|---|
| 1 July | Goods bought on credit for $77 from Youssef. |
| 3 July | Goods bought on credit for $54 from Mila. |
| 9 July | We return goods to Youssef worth $14. |
| 14 July | We pay Mila by cheque for the full $54. |
| 15 July | We settle our account with Youssef by a cash payment of $20. |

**5** Prepare the double entry accounts of Surinder and balance them at 30 September 2018.

| | |
|---|---|
| 1 September | Owner places $900 of her own money into the business bank account. |
| 3 September | Goods purchased on credit from Oscar for $102. |
| 6 September | Goods purchased on credit from Wassane for $75. |
| 10 September | Sales made on credit to Gabriela for $99. |
| 13 September | Owner returns goods worth $34 to Wassane. |
| 19 September | Commission received $65 cash. |
| 22 September | Sales made on credit to Khatia for $318. |
| 25 September | Khatia returns $58 of the goods that he purchased. |
| 26 September | Owner withdraws $100 from the bank for own private use. |
| 27 September | Cash received totalling $50 from Gabriela. |
| 29 September | Wages paid by cheque $240. |

**6** Prepare the ledger account of Anit and balance it at the month's end.

| | |
|---|---|
| 1 December | Sold goods on credit to Anit worth $800. |
| 4 December | Goods returned by Anit worth $75. |
| 10 December | Sale on credit to Anit worth $1200. |
| 18 December | Cheque received from Anit for $700. |
| 29 December | We accept a computer from Anit for business use – at an agreed valuation of $350. |

## Stretch

**7** If a business sells goods for more than they originally cost, surely the accounting equation will no longer hold. How do you think this issue is resolved?

**8** When a set of accounts are balanced for a period of time, the total of all the debit balances is always equal to the total of all the credit balances on the accounts. Explain why this is the case.

# Unit review

1   A furniture retailer buys tables for cash for use in the main office of the business. Which entry would record this correctly in the accounts?

| Account to be debited | Account to be credited |
|---|---|
| A  Purchases | Cash |
| B  Cash | Purchases |
| C  Office furniture | Cash |
| D  Cash | Office furniture |

2   Machinery bought on credit from Meghwar for resale had to be returned because it was unsuitable. The correct entry to record this in the accounts would be:

| Account to be debited | Account to be credited |
|---|---|
| A  Machinery | Meghwar |
| B  Meghwar | Purchases returns |
| C  Purchases returns | Meghwar |
| D  Meghwar | Machinery |

3   A sole trader takes equipment out of the business for her own use. The double entry transaction needed to record this would be:

| Account to be debited | Account to be credited |
|---|---|
| A  Owner's equity | Equipment |
| B  Equipment | Drawings |
| C  Equipment | Owner's equity |
| D  Drawings | Equipment |

4   The following account is balanced on 15 March 2018. What is the balance on the account on this date?

| Amir account | | | | | |
|---|---|---|---|---|---|
| 2018 | | $ | 2018 | | $ |
| 1 March | Balances b/d | 500 | 12 March | Cash | 250 |
| 7 April | Sales | 450 | 22 March | Sales returns | 75 |

A $700 debit          B $625 credit          C $700 debit          D $625 debit

# 2.2 Business documents

## Check your progress

| | ▲ | ▲▲ | ▲▲▲ |
|---|---|---|---|
| recognise and understand the following business documents: invoice, debit note, credit note, statement of account, cheque, receipt | | | |
| complete pro-forma business documents | | | |
| understand the use of business documents as sources of information: invoice, credit note, cheque counterfoil, paying-in slip, receipt, bank statement. | | | |

## Support

1   Match each of the following business documents to the account that is affected by the document. Each account should be matched to only one document.

| Business document | Account affected |
|---|---|
| **(a)** Sales invoice | Cash |
| **(b)** Cheque counterfoil | Sales returns |
| **(c)** Purchases invoice | Sales |
| **(d)** Credit note | Purchases |
| **(e)** Receipt | Bank |

## Practice

2   Complete this invoice by filling in the total column.

| DS BATHROOM DESIGN | L Boaler<br>31 Seagrave Road<br>CARCHESTER<br>CR1 7TG | | INVOICE | |
|---|---|---|---|---|
| To:<br>Claude<br>12 Hollins Street<br>CARCHESTER<br>CR8 0RD | | | Invoice number: **013**<br>Date: **1 June 2018** | |
| **Quantity** | **Description** | **Unit Price ($)** | **Total ($)** | |
| 40 | A4 Lever arch files | 1.20 | ___ | |
| 60 | Exercise books (A5) | 0.40 | ___ | |
| 200 | Pens (blue ink) | 0.20 | ___ | |
| Less 10% trade discount | | | ___ | |
| **TOTAL** | | | ___ | |

**3** Fill out the following cheque based on a payment of $650 to Sampson on 14 September 2018. The cheque will be paid out of your bank account.

| Date: | **Nanchester Bank** | Date: |
| _/_/_ | High Street Branch | _/_/_ |
| | | $ |
| Payee | Pay_____ | |
| _____ | _____ | |
| Amount: | _____ | _____ |
| $ | Cheque number    Branch sort code    Account no. | |
| A/C: 1448908 | 00025             04-01-26          1448908 | |

**4** Draw up an invoice with full details based on the following information:

- Your business name and address: Miguel sandwich shop, 31 Head Street, Oldtown, OT4 1SN
- Customer name and address: Hamman Business Conferences, Unit 12, Business Park, Oldtown, OT4 7XJ
- Details of sale: 50 mixed vegetarian sandwiches ($1.20 each), 25 fish sandwiches ($1.40 each), 20 savoury platters ($3 each) (order placed on 11 May 2018)
- Discount: Trade discount of 10%.

## Stretch

**5** Research online to find examples of online services that produce business documents that are designed specifically for a business's own needs? Do you think all businesses would use online packages to design their own set of documents?

## Unit review

**1** For which of the following accounts does a paying-in slip provide information for making debit entries?

**A** Credit suppliers      **C** Cash

**B** Credit customers      **D** Bank

**2** A statement of account does not contain details of which of the following?

**A** Amounts owing to the business by customers

**B** Amounts received in payment from customers

**C** Wages paid to workers who deliver goods to customers

**D** Details of goods received as returns from customers

**3** A cash sale for immediate payment may be recorded from which of the following business documents?

**A** Purchases invoice      **C** Debit note

**B** Receipt      **D** Credit note

**4** Which of the following documents normally results in an entry in the sales ledger?

**A** Bank statement      **C** Credit note

**B** Statement of account      **D** Cheque counterfoil

# 2.3 Books of prime entry

## Check your progress

Read the unit objectives below. Tick the column that best describes your progress in each.

| | ▲ | ▲▲ | ▲▲▲ |
|---|---|---|---|
| explain the advantage of using various books of prime entry | | | |
| explain the use of, and process, accounting data in the books of prime entry – cash book, petty cash book, sales journal, purchases journal, sales returns journal, purchases returns journal and the general journal | | | |
| post the ledger entries from the books of prime entry | | | |
| distinguish between and account for trade discount and cash discounts | | | |
| explain the dual function of the cash book as a book of prime entry and as a ledger account for bank and cash | | | |
| explain the use of and record payments and receipts made by bank transfers and other electronic means | | | |
| explain and apply the imprest system of petty cash. | | | |

## Support

1   Decide whether the following statements are true or false.

   (a)  All cash and bank transactions appear in the cash book.

   (b)  All sales of inventory appear in the sales journal.

   (c)  Anything sold on credit appears in the general journal.

   (d)  Goods returned by customers appear in the sales returns journal.

   (e)  Introduction of owner's equity will always appear in the general journal.

2   For each of the following, state in which journal you would record the transaction.

   (a)  Sale of goods on credit

   (b)  Owner's van brought into business for business use

   (c)  Car purchased on credit for business use

   (d)  Inventory purchased on credit

   (e)  Inventory sent back to original supplier due to its unsuitability

3   Use the following information to prepare a cash book for the month of March 2018.

   Balances on 1 March: Bank $320 (Dr) and Cash $60 (Dr)

   | 2 March | Received cheque from Shanaya for $560 |
   | 6 March | Sold goods for cash $50 |
   | 9 March | Paid Sorin by cheque $110 |
   | 15 March | Paid wages by cheque $250 |
   | 18 March | Received $88 commission in cash |
   | 21 March | Purchased goods for $440, paid immediately by cheque |
   | 25 March | Paid telephone expenses by cash $32 |

**Practice**

**4** The following is a summary of the petty cash transactions for June 2018.

| 1 June | Received from petty cashier as petty cash float | $100 |
|---|---|---|
| 2 June | Rail fares | $21 |
| 7 June | Bus fares | $9 |
| 10 June | Paper for printer | $6 |
| 15 June | Bus fares | $5 |
| 22 June | Pens and pencils | $12 |
| 29 June | Petrol | $27 |

(a) Prepare a petty cash book with columns for expenditure on travel and office supplies to record the month's transactions.

(b) Enter the necessary amount to restore the imprest and carry down the balance for the following month.

**5** Prepare a cash book for November 2018 from the following information.

1 Nov    Balances at the start of the month: Cash in hand $29 and bank overdraft $210

5 Nov    The following customers paid their accounts by cheque, in each case deducting 2.5% cash discounts (the amounts are pre-discounts):

        Isidore $560              Irina $320

9 Nov    Paid rent $285 by cheque

16 Nov    Withdrew $70 from bank for cash till

20 Nov    The following invoices are settled by cheque with the suppliers each allowing a 5% discount (the invoice total is pre-discount):

        Rajinder $400          Nelu $640

21 Nov    Cash purchases $44

24 Nov    Cash sales $111

28 Nov    Cash of $50 deposited into the bank

**6** Prepare the journal entries and double entry accounts to record the following transactions.

1 June    Goods sold on credit to Farzana for $230

9 June    Goods sold on credit to Julien for $155

13 June    Goods purchased on credit from Khamisi for $47

20 June    Goods sold on credit to Farzana for $101

24 June    Goods purchased on credit from Vendula for $95

**7** Prepare the journal entries to record the following transactions.

1 Oct    Sold machinery on credit to Amerdeep for $560

5 Oct    Owner's van valued at $5200 is brought into the business

13 Oct    Debt of $80 owing to business is transferred from Horaci to Gerda

19 Oct    Business transfers a computer to Clemente in return for cancellation of $400 debt owed to him by business

23 Oct    Equipment bought on credit from Eduard for $290

## Stretch

8    Prepare the journal entries and double entry accounts to record the following transactions. Then transfer the monthly totals to the accounts in the nominal ledger.

|  |  |
|---|---|
| 1 July | Goods purchased on credit from Stefano for $86 |
| 3 July | Goods purchased on credit from Yannick for $63 |
| 5 July | Credit sales for $314 to Natalia |
| 7 July | Goods worth $31 are returned to Stefano |
| 10 July | Natalia returns goods worth $31 |
| 15 July | Credit purchases from Proclus for $92 |
| 19 July | Sales made on credit to Dian for $167 |
| 20 July | Goods returned to Proclus valued at $19 |
| 25 July | Goods sold to Dian for $182 |
| 28 July | Dian returns goods worth $41 |

## Unit review

1    Where is the purchases account located?

A  Purchases journal                    C  General journal

B  Purchases ledger                     D  Nominal ledger

2    Which of the following transactions is recorded in the sales returns journal?

A  Goods sent back to the business by customers

B  Sales of inventory

C  Equipment used in the business that must be returned

D  Inventory returned to the credit supplier

3    Credit purchases of tables for resale by a furniture retailer are recorded in which book of prime entry?

A  Cash book                            C  Purchases journal

B  General journal                      D  Petty cash book

4    Equipment used in a business is returned to the original supplier. In which book of prime entry is this recorded?

A  General journal                      C  Purchases journal

B  Cash book                            D  Purchases returns journal

# Chapter 2 review

1   The account is balanced on 30 April 2018. What is the account's balance on this date?

| Gita account | | | | | |
|---|---|---|---|---|---|
| | | $ | | | $ |
| 12 April | Purchases returns | 55 | 1 April | Balance b/d | 290 |
| 16 April | Bank | 420 | 7 April | Purchases | 450 |

   **A** $740 credit                          **C** $265 credit
   **B** $740 debit                           **D** $265 debit

2   Goods are sold on credit by Gakahr but returned by Kamboh. Which entry would record this correctly in the accounts?

| | Account to be debited | Account to be credited |
|---|---|---|
| **A** | Kamboh | Purchases returns |
| **B** | Sales returns | Kamboh |
| **C** | Sales returns | Gakahr |
| **D** | Sales | Kamboh |

3   Which of the following is classed as an asset?

   **A** Inventory purchased on credit          **C** Amounts owing to credit suppliers
   **B** Money owing to the bank                **D** Short-term bank loan

4   Which is the correct double entry to record paying insurance from the business bank account?

| | Account to be debited | Account to be credited |
|---|---|---|
| **A** | Bank | Insurance |
| **B** | Insurance | Bank |
| **C** | Purchases | Bank |
| **D** | Insurance | Cash |

5   Which of the following would not be recorded in the sales account?

   **A** Sale of goods for cash                 **C** Sale of goods on credit
   **B** Sale of services                        **D** Sale of items used in business

6   Which of the following business documents does not generate an entry in the cash book?

   **A** Cheque counterfoil                     **C** Sales invoice
   **B** Receipt                                 **D** Paying-in slip

7   Where would the account of credit customers be found?

   **A** Sales ledger                            **C** General journal
   **B** Sales journal                           **D** Nominal ledger

8   Which of the following transactions is entered in the general journal?

   **A** Cash introduced into the business by the owner
   **B** Car used for business purchased on credit
   **C** Goods sold on credit that are returned by the customer
   **D** Small items of cash payments

9  Which of the following best describes the imprest system?

   A  A system where cash and bank transactions are recorded within the same account
   B  The transfer of money between cash and bank accounts
   C  Ensuring that petty cash is always maintained at the same amount at the start of each period
   D  Using several columns to record separate categories of expenditure

10  Which of the following statements is true?

   A  Cash discounts are not recorded in the ledger accounts
   B  Trade discounts are given for prompt payment
   C  Discounts allowed are given to credit suppliers
   D  Discounts received are debited to the accounts of credit suppliers

11  For each of the following transactions, state which side and in which account it should be recorded. The first one has been done for you.                                              [12]

| | Account to be debited | Account to be credited |
|---|---|---|
| (a)  Wages paid from bank account | Wages | Bank |
| (b)  Car purchased on credit from Bhutta | | |
| (c)  Inventory sent back by business to Sahi | | |
| (d)  Rent received in cash | | |
| (e)  Cash paid into business bank account | | |
| (f)  Sale of inventory on credit to Viktor | | |
| (g)  Owner takes money out of bank for personal use | | |

A  Use the following information to prepare the double entry account of Kassar for the month of March 2018. Balance the account for the end of the month.                              [7]

   (a)  1 March     Balance on account was a credit balance of $720
   (b)  5 March     Purchases made on credit from Kassar for $2230
   (c)  18 March    Payment made to Kassar from bank of $1800
   (d)  24 March    Goods returned to Kassar valued at $380
   (e)  26 March    Purchases made on credit from Kassar for $490
   (f)  28 March    A further payment is made to Kassar from the business bank account for $400

| Kassar | | | | | |
|---|---|---|---|---|---|
| 2018 | | $ | 2018 | | $ |
| | | | 1 March | Balance b/d | 720 |

B  In which ledger would you find the account of Kassar?                                      [1]

                                                                              [Total 20]

**12 A** Use the following details to prepare a cash book for the month of May 2018. **[16]**

  **(a)** 1 May   Opening balances as follows: Bank $1250; Cash $88

  **(b)** 3 May   Purchases of $152 paid for by cheque

  **(c)** 5 May   Commission received in cash $45

  **(d)** 8 May   Payments by cheque to credit suppliers on invoice totals as follows:

    Bernat $320

    Julia $120

    A 5% discount is given by both credit suppliers.

  **(e)** 12 May   Payment received by cheque for $344 from a credit customer, Sahar. The payment is for an invoice totalling $370, that is, the difference represents discounts allowed.

  **(f)** 14 May   Cash taken by the owner $50

  **(g)** 24 May   Cheques sent to credit suppliers as follows:

    To Juan for an invoice total of $400

    To Ariel for an invoice total of $200

    In each case, a discount on the invoice of 2.5% is given by the supplier.

**B** State two reasons why a business would choose to maintain a cash book and a petty cash book at the same time. **[2]**

**C** State which ledger the totals for discounts allowed and received would be posted to at the end of the month. **[1]**

**D** Give one reason why businesses allow customers trade credit. **[1]**

**[Total 20]**

**13 A** Prepare the journal entries necessary to record the following transactions. Narratives are not required. **[11]**

  **(a)** 4 April   Equipment worth $2500 is exchanged with a friend for a machine of equivalent value

  **(b)** 8 April   We are owed $900 by Hania. She has a cash flow shortage so gives us half of the amount owing in cash with the remaining balance settled by giving the business a computer for business use

  **(c)** 17 April   Owner transfers a personal item of office furniture into business use at the value of $400

  **(d)** 23 April   Fixtures and fittings bought on credit from Bulan for $250

  **(e)** 25 April   Car taken out of business for personal use was valued at $5300

**B** Complete the following table. The first one has been done for you. **[9]**

| Business document | Account to be debited | Account to be credited | Recorded in the following book of prime entry |
|---|---|---|---|
| (a) Cheque counterfoil showing cheque written to Igor | I Dicken | Bank (or cash book) | Cash book |
| (b) Sales invoice sent to Miron | | | |
| (c) Paying-in slip for cheque deposited from Nyoman | | | |
| (d) Credit note sent to Caesar | | | |

# 3 Verification of accounting records

## 3.1 The trial balance

### Check your progress

| Read the unit objectives below. Tick the column that best describes your progress in each. | ▲ | ▲▲ | ▲▲▲ |
|---|---|---|---|
| understand that a trial balance is a statement of ledger balances on a particular date | | | |
| outline the uses and limitations of a trial balance | | | |
| prepare a trial balance from a given list of balances and amend a trial balance which contains errors | | | |
| identify and explain those errors which do not affect the trial balance – commission, compensating, complete reversal, omission, original entry, principle. | | | |

### Support

1    Decide whether the following are debit or credit balances in the trial balance.

   (a) Premises
   (b) Cash
   (c) Trade receivables
   (d) Trade payables
   (e) Opening inventory
   (f) Owner's equity

2    State whether the following are true or false.

   (a) The trial balance will always balance.
   (b) The bank balance can appear in either the debit or credit column of a trial balance.
   (c) The cash balance can appear in either the debit or credit column of a trial balance.
   (d) Owner's equity is the debit column of a trial balance.
   (e) Opening inventory always appears underneath a trial balance.

### Practice

3    Identify the type of error made in each of the following transactions.

   (a) A payment to Riya of $45 by cheque was missed out of the double entry accounts.
   (b) Rent received of $560 paid into the bank was mistakenly entered as $650 in both accounts.
   (c) Computer maintenance expenses of $88 was debited to the computer account.
   (d) Cash of $12 received from Draha was debited to Draha and credited to the cash account.
   (e) A cheque for $99 received from Zaman was credited in error to the account of Zeinab.

**4** Use the following balances to prepare a trial balance for the end of year.

| | $ |
|---|---|
| Sales | 41480 |
| Wages and salaries | 5600 |
| Purchases | 26790 |
| Discounts received | 300 |
| Inventory as at 1 Jan 2018 | 1015 |
| Inventory as at 31 Dec 2018 | 999 |
| Office expenses | 1875 |
| Vehicles | 6600 |
| Owner's equity | 9000 |
| Equipment | 8900 |

**5** A trial balance has been prepared for Wayan. It contains errors. Use the following information to prepare a corrected trial balance as at 31 December 2018.

| Wayan Trial balance for the year ended 31 December 2018 | | |
|---|---|---|
| | Dr | Cr |
| | $ | $ |
| Sales | 48900 | |
| Purchases | | 13726 |
| Sales returns | 411 | |
| Purchases returns | | 238 |
| Motor vehicles | | 17500 |
| Discounts received | 340 | |
| Office expenses | | 14500 |
| Office equipment | 25940 | |
| Inventory at 1 January 2018 | 8312 | |
| Inventory at 31 December 2018 | 5670 | |
| Trade payables | | 7681 |
| Trade receivables | 10190 | |
| Bank | 756 | |
| Office salaries | | 22300 |
| Discounts allowed | | 564 |
| Owner's equity | 66600 | |
| Drawings | 9560 | |
| Suspense | | |
| | 176679 | 76509 |

## Stretch

6    A business owner prepared a trial balance. Prepare an updated trial balance after the following transactions.

Machinery bought for $800, payment by cheque

Bank loan obtained for $2000

Owner takes $500 from the business bank account

Cheng is paid in full from the bank account

Bhavana pays business amount owed to business in cash

|  | Dr | Cr |
|---|---|---|
|  | $ | $ |
| Capital |  | 20000 |
| Machinery | 9500 |  |
| Bank | 5455 |  |
| Machinery insurance | 156 |  |
| Purchases | 990 |  |
| Ling |  | 55 |
| Returns outwards |  | 113 |
| Vehicle | 7557 |  |
| Cheng |  | 2100 |
| Sales |  | 1590 |
| Bhavana | 200 |  |
|  | 23858 | 23858 |

## Unit review

1    By how much would the following balance add to the credit column of a trial balance?

|  | $ |
|---|---|
| Owner's equity | 55400 |
| Drawings | 11950 |
| Trade payables | 320 |
| Office equipment | 18500 |
| Mortgage | 42600 |

A  $98320        B  $132770        C  $109950        D  $71670

2    Which of the following appears in the debit column of a trial balance?

A  Inventory at year end        C  Bank loan

B  Discounts received           D  Trade receivables

3    Which of the following is an example of an error of commission?

A  A payment received from a customer is debited to the bank and credited to the customer account.

B  A payment received from a customer is recorded in a different customer's account.

C  A payment received from a customer is incorrect in value.

D  A payment received from a customer is not recorded in the double entry accounts.

4    Wages of $540 are paid in cash. The entries made in the accounts are as follows: Debit: cash $540; Credit: Wages $540. What type of error has been made?

A  Compensating        C  Principle

B  Commission          D  Complete reversal

# 3.2 Correction of errors

## Check your progress

| Read the unit objectives below. Tick the column that best describes your progress in each. | ▲ | ▲▲ | ▲▲▲ |
|---|---|---|---|
| correct errors by means of journal entries | | | |
| explain the use of a suspense account as a temporary measure to balance the trial balance | | | |
| correct errors by means of suspense accounts | | | |
| adjust a profit or loss for an accounting period after the correction of errors | | | |
| understand the effect of correction of errors on a statement of financial position. | | | |

## Support

1   For each of the following transactions, state the type of error made.

(a)  Purchases returns of $87 was entered in both accounts as $870.

(b)  Sales on credit for $44 to Noor was debited to the account of Yarin.

(c)  Office expenses of $21 was actually a payment made for the owner's private expenses.

(d)  Purchases returns of $55 was debited to purchases returns and credited to trade payables.

2   For each of the following transactions, state the type of error made.

(a)  Payment of cash made for $56 for heating costs was missed out of the double entry accounts.

(b)  Sale of van used in business for $500 was credited to the sales account.

(c)  Sales of $48 cash were debited to sales and credited to cash.

(d)  Both discounts allowed and discounts received were overcast by $57.

3   For each of the following errors state whether the correction of the error requires an entry in a suspense account.

(a)  Purchases account overcast by $40

(b)  Drawings entered on credit side of account

(c)  Wages of $110 paid in cash entered in both accounts as $220

(d)  Sales returns of $90 entered in purchases returns in error

(e)  Payment received from trade receivables is debited to both accounts

## Practice

4   Prepare the general journal entries to record the correction of the following errors. Narratives are not required.

(a) Purchases of goods on credit for $112 from Thea were entered by mistake in the account of Tina.

(b) Return of a car previously sold by the business for $2000 was mistakenly treated as sales returns.

(c) A cheque received from Adrien for $72 was entered in both accounts as $27.

(d) Payment by cheque to Agatho of $103 was completely missed out.

(e) Purchases returns of $85 to Serge was debited to purchases returns and credited to Serge.

5   Prepare the general journal entries to record the correction of the following errors. Narratives are not required.

(a) Insurance paid in cash for $52 was entered in both accounts as $43.

(b) Sale on credit to Georgia for $110 was debited to sales and credited to the customer's account.

(c) Rent received of $320 by cheque was missed out from the ledgers.

(d) Heating costs paid by cheque for $450 included costs totalling $150 belonging to the owner's private house.

(e) Wages paid of $290 cash was entered in both accounts as $390.

6   A trial balance has different totals for each column. There was a $479 shortage on the credit column and a suspense account was opened. The following errors were soon discovered. Prepare the general journal entries and, if appropriate the entries in the suspense account to record the correction of the following errors.

(a) Rent paid by cheque for $150 was entered on the debit sides of both accounts.

(b) Payment to Durga for $24 cash was entered in both accounts as $42.

(c) Sales returns from Rashmi worth $45 was entered in Rashmi account on the debit side.

(d) Purchases returns was undercast by $89.

7   A loss for the year was calculated as $55. However, shortly afterwards the following errors were found. Calculate the net profit (or loss) once all the errors have been corrected.

(a) Discounts allowed was overcast by $335.

(b) Inventory taken by the owner of the business for private use valued at $33 was not recorded.

(c) Purchase of inventory for $450 was treated as the purchase of a non-current asset.

(d) Wages of $100 was omitted from the accounts.

## Stretch

8   A trial balance does not balance and a suspense account was opened. After investigation, the following errors were discovered.

Discounts received of $75 was accounted for in the general ledger account as if it were discounts allowed.

Rent paid by cheque of $560 was entered in the rent account correctly but in the bank account as an income of $56.

Purchases of $145 on credit from Cirili was only entered in the personal account.

Prepare the general journal entries and, if appropriate the entries in the suspense account to record the correction of the following errors. Calculate the initial discrepancy from the trial balance.

**9** Profit for the year is calculated as $250. However, the following errors were discovered.

Sales account is undercast by $109.

General expenses of $45 was credited to the account by mistake.

Phone expenses paid by cheque for $64 included a private phone payment of $17.

Purchase on credit for $77 from Osanna was entered in both accounts as $177.

(a) Prepare the entries in the general journal to record the correction of these errors.

(b) Prepare a suspense account to record the correction of these errors. Also calculate the correct opening balance on the suspense account.

(c) Prepare a statement of corrected net profit.

## Unit review

**1** Entering amounts into the wrong customer's account is what type of error?

| | |
|---|---|
| A Omission | C Original entry |
| B Commission | D Principle |

**2** Entering an incorrect amount for both the debit and credit entries of a transaction is what type of error?

| | |
|---|---|
| A Principle | C Complete reversal |
| B Compensating | D Original entry |

**3** Which of the following errors is corrected with an entry in a suspense account?

A Entering double the correct amount for both entries

B Making an entry in the wrong type of account on the correct side

C Missing out the debit entry for a transaction

D Missing out the debt and credit entries for a transaction

**4** Which of the following errors would not affect the profit for the year?

A Entering a payment for wages on the credit side of the wages account

B Completely missing out the entries for cash drawings

C Classing the sale of an asset as a sale of inventory

D Overcasting discounts allowed

# 3.3 Bank reconciliation

## Check your progress

| Read the unit objectives below. Tick the column that best describes your progress in each. | ▲ | ▲▲ | ▲▲▲ |
|---|---|---|---|
| understand the use and purpose of a bank statement | | | |
| update the cash book for bank charges, bank interest paid and received, correction of errors, credit transfers, direct debits, dividends, and standing orders | | | |
| understand the purpose of, and prepare, a bank reconciliation statement to include bank errors, uncredited deposits and unpresented cheques. | | | |

## Support

1   Decide whether the following are debit and credit entries in a cash book.

   **(a)** Credit transfers        **(d)** Dividends received       **(g)** Bank charges

   **(b)** Standing orders         **(e)** Interest received        **(h)** Dishonoured cheques

   **(c)** Interest paid           **(f)** Direct debits

2   The following cash book was completed for November 2018.

| | | Cash book | | | |
|---|---|---|---|---|---|
| | | $ | | | $ |
| 1 Nov | Balance b/d | 99 | 8 Nov | Howard | 367 |
| 10 Nov | Erasto | 414 | 15 Nov | Hermann | 139 |
| 19 Nov | Louis | 240 | 30 Nov | Balance c/d | 247 |
| | | 753 | | | 753 |

The following items are on the bank statement for November but have not been entered in the cash book.

| | $ |
|---|---|
| Interest paid | 12 |
| Direct debits paid | 310 |
| Credit transfer received | 250 |

Prepare the updated cash book.

## Practice

3 The following cash book was completed for March 2018.

| | | $ | | | $ |
|---|---|---|---|---|---|
| | | **Cash book** | | | |
| 1 Mar | Balance b/d | 314 | 2 Mar | Yasmin | 232 |
| 3 Mar | Francesca | 545 | 11 Mar | Rong | 414 |
| 12 Mar | Pietro | 766 | 21 Mar | Yezekael | 505 |
| 24 Mar | Vavara | | 31 Mar | Balance c/d | 474 |
| | | 1625 | | | 1625 |
| 1 Apr | Balance b/d | 474 | | | |

The following items are on the bank statement for March but have not been entered in the cash book.

| | $ |
|---|---|
| Interest paid | 34 |
| Direct debit: electricity | 130 |
| Dividends received | 45 |
| Standing order: Zikmund | 290 |
| Bank charges | 36 |
| Credit transfer: Myron | 350 |

Prepare the updated cash book.

4 On 30 June 2018, Sebastian cash book is brought up to date and now has a debit balance of $116. However, the balance on the bank statement is still different from this updated cash book balance. Unpresented cheques paid out amounted to $564 and uncredited deposits total $670. No errors are present.

Prepare a bank reconciliation statement and calculate the balance on the bank statement.

5 Javed has updated his cash book which now has a debit balance of $89.45. There is still a discrepancy between the updated cash book balance and the bank statement balance. On the same date, the bank statement shows an overdrawn balance of $75.66.

The following information is available.

| | |
|---|---|
| Unpresented cheque 100341 | $40.11 |
| Unpresented cheque 100344 | $91.14 |
| Uncredited deposit from Hassan | $296.36 |

Produce a bank reconciliation statement to show that the discrepancy between the two balances can be explained by timing differences.

6   Use the cash book and bank statement for June to prepare an updated cash book and a bank reconciliation statement as at 30 June 2018.

| Cash book | | | | | |
|---|---|---|---|---|---|
| | | $ | | | $ |
| 1 June | Balance b/d | 38 | 16 June | Roberto | 266 |
| 9 June | Jon | 390 | 24 June | Olaf | 177 |
| 18 June | Bertran | 119 | 30 June | Balance b/d | 104 |
| | | 547 | | | 547 |

| Bank statement | | Payments | Receipts | Balance |
|---|---|---|---|---|
| | | $ | $ | $ |
| 1 June | Balance b/d | | | 38 |
| 12 June | Cheque deposited | | 390 | 428 |
| 17 June | Interest | | 12 | 440 |
| 19 June | Standing order | 65 | | 375 |
| 22 June | Cheque 1011 | 266 | | 109 |
| 26 June | Direct debit | 47 | | 62 |
| 30 June | Balance at month end | | | 62 |

## Stretch

7   Liddle received a bank statement for July 2018 showing an overdrawn balance of $363 at the end of the month. The bank column of her cash book had a debit balance of $90 on 1 July. A comparison of the cash book and the bank statement revealed the following.

Items appearing only on the bank statement:
- Interest paid $19
- Direct debit to WestCo $95
- Gas bill paid by standing order $105
- Credit transfer received of $260
- Cheque received from Hyun-jun, a credit customer, for $125 was dishonoured

Items appearing only in the cash book:

Cheques paid to credit suppliers:
- Ana $335
- Emil $210

Cheques received from credit customers:
- Alexandra $615
- Efrem $219

The total of the debit side of the cash book had been overcast by $80.

Prepare the cash book of Liddle as at 31 July 2018. Then prepare a bank reconciliation statement for the same date.

# Unit review

1   Which of the following is found on the debit side of the cash book?

   **A**  Direct debit payment            **C**  Standing order payments

   **B**  Dishonoured cheques             **D**  Interest received

2   Which of the following is not an automated transaction?

   **A**  Unpresented cheque              **C**  Credit transfer

   **B**  Bank charges                     **D**  Standing order

3   Look at the cash book.

| Cash book | | | |
|---|---|---|---|
| | $ | | $ |
| TWC Ltd | 56 | Artem | 72 |
| Parker | 43 | Jun-suh | 11 |

The following two items are on the bank statement but not yet in the cash book.

Interest received $5

Dishonoured cheque $99

What is the balance on the cash book after it has been updated?

   **A**  $16 debit                      **C**  $120 debit

   **B**  $21 debit                      **D**  $78 credit

4   A cheque which a bank will not process due to it being unpresented for a long period is known as a:

   **A**  Dishonoured cheque             **C**  Stale cheque

   **B**  Bouncing cheque                **D**  Dated cheque

# 3.4 Control accounts

## Check your progress

Read the unit objectives below. Tick the column that best describes your progress in each.

| | ▲ | ▲ | ▲ |
|---|---|---|---|
| understand the purposes of purchases ledger and sales ledger control accounts | | | |
| identify the books of prime entry as sources of information for the control account entries | | | |
| prepare purchases ledger and sales ledger control accounts to include credit purchases and sales, receipts and payments, cash discounts, returns, irrecoverable debts, dishonoured cheques, interest on overdue accounts, contra entries, refunds, and opening and closing balances (debit and credit within each account). | | | |

## Support

**1**   Use the following information to prepare a sales ledger control account.

| | $ |
|---|---|
| Trade receivables at the start of the month | 421 |
| Trade receivables at the end of the month | 556 |
| Credit sales for the month | 2341 |
| Bank | 2010 |
| Sales returns | 78 |
| Discounts allowed | 23 |
| Irrecoverable debts | 95 |

**2**   Use the following information to prepare a purchases ledger control account.

| | $ |
|---|---|
| Balance of trade payables at start of month | 890 |
| Balance of trade payables at end of month | 1010 |
| Credit purchases | 10005 |
| Bank payments to trade payables | 9201 |
| Discounts received | 230 |
| Purchases returns | 454 |

## Practice

**3** Prepare a purchases ledger control account using the following information.

| | $ |
|---|---|
| Balance of trade payables at 1 November | 10190 |
| Balance of trade payables at 30 November | 9807 |
| Total credit purchases for month | 146550 |
| Payments in respect of trade payables | 141411 |
| Purchases returns for November | 2400 |
| Discounts received in November | 3122 |

**4** Prepare a sales ledger control account using the following information.

| | $ |
|---|---|
| Balance of trade receivables at 1 November | 21406 |
| Balance of trade receivables at 30 November | 19760 |
| Total credit sales for month | 234000 |
| Payments received from trade receivables | 224009 |
| Sales returns for November | 5109 |
| Discounts allowed in November | 6101 |
| Irrecoverable debts | 875 |
| Dishonoured cheques | 448 |

**5** Prepare a sales ledger control account using the following information.

| | $ |
|---|---|
| Balance of trade receivables at 1 November | 2480 |
| Balance of trade receivables at 30 November | 4179 |
| Total credit sales for month | 54234 |
| Payments received from trade receivables | 48800 |
| Sales returns for November | 1870 |
| Discounts allowed in November | 1020 |
| Contra entries in sales ledger | 460 |
| Interest on overdue accounts from customers | 0 |
| Irrecoverable debts | 985 |
| Dishonoured cheques | 140 |

**6** Prepare a purchases ledger control account using the following information.

| | $ |
|---|---|
| Balance of trade payables at 1 November | 1314 |
| Balance of trade payables at 30 November | 1910 |
| Total credit purchases for month | 22410 |
| Payments in respect of trade payables | 21010 |
| Purchases returns for November | 311 |
| Discounts received in November | 448 |
| Contra entries in purchases ledger | 101 |
| Interest on overdue accounts owing to suppliers | 56 |

## Stretch

7 The following information was taken from the sales and purchases ledgers of a business. The chief accountant suspects that a junior worker has taken some of the cash received from customers in respect of credit sales for his own use without authorisation. The chief accountant believes the amount is probably close to $500. Prepare control accounts for the purchases and sales ledgers for May 2018 and advise the chief accountant if his suspicions are correct.

| | $ |
|---|---|
| Sales ledger balances as at 1 May 2018 | 4141 |
| Purchases ledger balances as at 1 May 2018 | 2418 |
| Debit balances in purchases ledger as at 1 May 2018 | 111 |
| Credit sales | 78999 |
| Credit purchases | 34387 |
| Cash book receipts in respect of credit sales | 70900 |
| Cash book payments for credit purchases | 32990 |
| Dishonoured cheques | 290 |
| Contra entries | 187 |
| Sales returns | 441 |
| Purchases returns | 341 |
| Irrecoverable debts | 1250 |
| Refunds to customers | 88 |
| Discounts allowed | 770 |
| Discounts received | 300 |
| Sales ledger balances as at 31 May 2018 | 9461 |
| Purchases ledger balances as at 31 May 2018 | 2876 |

8 The following information was taken from the sales and purchases ledgers of a business. The balances at the end of August 2018 cannot be located. Prepare control accounts for the sales and purchases ledgers to calculate the missing balances. It is assumed no other errors are present.

| | $ |
|---|---|
| Sales ledger balances as at 1 August | 4152 |
| Purchases ledger balances as at 1 August | 3123 |
| Credit sales for August | 177800 |
| Credit purchases for August | 101450 |
| Cash sales | 15524 |
| Cash purchases | 12311 |
| Cash and bank receipts in respect of credit sales | 168045 |
| Dishonoured cheques | 890 |
| Credit balances in sales ledger as at 1 August | 282 |
| Contra entries | 660 |
| Returns inwards | 1317 |
| Bad debts | 2450 |
| Payments made for credit purchases | 95670 |
| Refunds to customers | 111 |
| Interest on overdue accounts owed to suppliers | 78 |
| Discounts allowed | 1291 |
| Discounts received | 678 |
| Returns outwards | 850 |
| Sales ledger balances as at 31 August | ? |
| Purchases ledger balances as at 31 August | ? |

# Unit review

**1**  Which of the following appears on the debit side of the sales ledger control account?

   **A** Sales returns          **B** Cash sales          **C** Credit sales          **D** Contra entries

**2**  Which of the following appears on the credit side of the purchases ledger control account?

   **A** Interest owing on late payments to suppliers          **C** Cash purchases

   **B** Contra entries          **D** Payments for trade payables

**3**  Use the following information to calculate the value of credit sales for the period.

| | $ |
|---|---|
| Trade receivables at start of period | 414 |
| Trade receivables at end of period | 542 |
| Payments from trade receivables | 24 511 |
| Sales returns | 766 |

   **A** $23 617          **B** $23 873          **C** $24 639          **D** $26 233

**4**  Use the following information to calculate the value of credit purchases for the period.

| | $ |
|---|---|
| Trade payables at start of period | 651 |
| Trade payables at end of period | 711 |
| Payments to trade payables | 34 343 |
| Discounts received | 560 |

   **A** $36 265          **B** $34 403          **C** $33 723          **D** $33 843

# Chapter 3 review

**1** Which of the following appears in the credit column of the trial balance?

  **A** Trade receivables        **C** Bank overdraft

  **B** Petty cash        **D** Drawings

**2** When entering a transaction, double the amount intended is entered in both accounts on the correct sides. This is an example of which type of error?

  **A** Complete reversal        **C** Compensating

  **B** Commission        **D** Original entry

**3** Which of the following statements is not true?

  **A** Errors of commission do not affect profit.

  **B** Suspense accounts have no outstanding balance once all errors have been corrected.

  **C** If the suspense account has no outstanding balance then all errors have been found.

  **D** Errors of complete reversal are corrected by appropriate entries on the opposite side of each account.

**4** Which of the following errors would be corrected with a credit entry in a suspense account?

  **A** Purchases are undercast

  **B** Payment to credit supplier is missed out of supplier's account

  **C** Entry in sales account is overcast

  **D** Receipt of money is missed out of cash book

**5** Which of the following errors would result in profit being overstated?

  **A** Entering a payment of trade payables twice by mistake

  **B** Purchases returns account is overcast

  **C** Sales returns account is undercast

  **D** Drawings account is overcast

**6** Which of the following is debited to a cash book when bringing it up to date?

  **A** Direct debit payments        **C** Standing orders

  **B** Interest received        **D** Dishonoured cheques

**7** Once a cash book has been brought up to date, which of the following would not explain any difference between the cash book balance and the bank statement balance on the same date?

  **A** Unpresented cheques        **C** Credit transfers

  **B** Fraud        **D** Uncredited deposits

**8** Which of the following appears on the debit side of the sales ledger control account?

  **A** Cash sales        **C** Discounts allowed

  **B** Dishonoured cheques        **D** Sales returns

**9** Which of the following does not appear in a purchases ledger control account?

  **A** Credit purchases        **C** Purchases returns

  **B** Refunds to customers        **D** Payments to trade payables

10  Which of the following can appear in sales ledger and purchases ledger control accounts?

A  Contra entries                    C  Trade receivables balances

B  Cash sales                        D  Credit purchases

11  A trial balance prepared for Mirone on 30 June 2018 had the following totals for each column.

Debit column $145 670                    Credit column $147 485

In July 2018, the following errors are found.

(i)   Rent (expense) is entered in the account as a credit entry of $780. However, the correct entry for the rent expense is $540.

(ii)  Commission received of $715 is only entered in the cash book.

(iii) The purchases returns journal is undercast by $215.

(iv)  Mirone deposited $1230 of his own money into the business bank account. This is credited to the sales account in error.

A  Name the type of error made in (iv)                                                    [1]

B  Prepare entries in the general journal required to correct these errors.               [8]

C  Open a suspense account and prepare the entries to correct the errors found.           [4]

D  Profit for the year was initially calculated as $6580. Calculate the profit for the year after making corrections for all the errors discovered.                                      [5]

E  A business manager claims that all errors must have been found, as there is no longer any outstanding balance on the suspense account as at 31 July 2018. Explain why this may not be true.                                                                         [2]

[Total 20]

12  The bank columns in the cash book of Dalitso for April 2018 and the bank statement for that month are shown below.

| Cash book (bank column only) | | | | | |
|---|---|---|---|---|---|
| 2018 | | $ | 2018 | | $ |
| 4 Apr | Deposit: Atalia | 110 | 1 Apr | Balance b/d | 176 |
| 13 Apr | Deposit: Teodora | 87 | 5 Apr | Marios | 45 |
| 15 Apr | Deposit: Darma | 123 | 20 Apr | Usman | 88 |
| 23 Apr | Deposit: Devdas | 280 | 24 Apr | Tiberiu | 155 |
| 25 Apr | Deposit: Amelia | 315 | 29 Apr | Balance c/d | 451 |
| | | 915 | | | 915 |

| Bank statement | | Dr | Cr | Balance |
|---|---|---|---|---|
| 2018 | | $ | $ | $ |
| 1 Apr | Balance b/d | | | 176 (Dr) |
| 8 Apr | 11334 | 45 | | 221 (Dr) |
| 9 Apr | Sundries | | 110 | 111 (Dr) |
| 11 Apr | Direct debit | 67 | | 178 (Dr) |
| 16 Apr | Standing order | 75 | | 253 (Dr) |
| 18 Apr | Sundries | | 87 | 166 (Dr) |
| 26 Apr | 11335 | 88 | | 254 (Dr) |
| 27 Apr | Sundries | | 123 | 131 (Dr) |
| 29 Apr | Dividends | | 25 | 106 (Dr) |

**A** Prepare the cash book as at 30 April 2018. [5]

**B** Prepare a bank reconciliation statement as at 30 April 2018. [6]

**C** Explain each of the following terms.

  **(i)** Dishonoured cheque [2]

  **(ii)** Direct debit [2]

  **(iii)** Standing order [2]

**D** State three possible explanations for why the bank statement and updated cash book balance cannot be reconciled. [3]

[Total 20]

13  There has been an accusation that a member of staff receiving cash receipts from customer payments is not depositing all the money into the business bank account, and the individual is taking some money without authorisation. It is suggested that control accounts could help to identify if fraud is occurring and how much money may have been embezzled.

| | $ |
|---|---|
| Sales ledger balances as at 1 July 2018 | 5422 |
| Purchases ledger balances as at 1 July 2018 | 3870 |
| Credit sales for July | 65780 |
| Credit purchases for July | 43005 |
| Cash and bank receipts in respect of credit sales | 59012 |
| Dishonoured cheques | 400 |
| Contra entries | 120 |
| Sales returns | 890 |
| Irrecoverable debts | 50 |
| Payments made for credit purchases | 40100 |
| Interest on overdue accounts owed to suppliers | 65 |
| Discounts allowed | 755 |
| Discounts received | 487 |
| Purchases returns | 289 |
| Sales ledger balances as at 31 July 2018 | 8775 |
| Purchases ledger balances as at 31 July 2018 | 5944 |

**A** Prepare a purchases ledger control account for July 2018. [8]

**B** Prepare a sales ledger control account for July 2018. [8]

**C** How much money has been taken without authorisation? [1]

**D** State in which book of prime entry the following information is located.

  **(i)** Dishonoured cheques [1]

  **(ii)** Irrecoverable debts [1]

**E** If a control account balances, state a type of error that may still exist in the accounts. [1]

[Total 20]

# 4 Accounting procedures

## 4.1 Capital and revenue expenditure and receipts

### Check your progress

| Read the unit objectives below. Tick the column that best describes your progress in each. | ▲ | ▲▲ | ▲▲▲ |
|---|---|---|---|
| distinguish between and account for capital expenditure and revenue expenditure | | | |
| distinguish between and account for capital receipts and revenue receipts | | | |
| calculate and comment on the effect on profit of incorrect treatment | | | |
| calculate and comment on the effect on asset valuations of incorrect treatment. | | | |

### Support

1   Decide whether the following are capital expenditure or revenue expenditure.

   (a) Purchase of furniture for business use
   (b) Purchase of kitchen equipment for resale
   (c) Repairs to premises
   (d) Enlarging premises
   (e) Wages of production workers
   (f) Purchase of car for use by sales manager

2   Decide whether the following are capital receipts or revenue receipts.

   (a) Sale of goods purchased for resale
   (b) Sale of business premises
   (c) Money placed in business bank account by owner
   (d) Money received from renting property
   (e) Bank loan paid into business account

3   Decide whether the following are capital expenditure, capital receipts, revenue expenditure or revenue receipts.

   (a) Sale of inventory
   (b) Sale of business premises
   (c) Wages paid to production workers
   (d) Annual marketing costs
   (e) Car purchased for resale
   (f) Bank loan taken by business

   (g) Purchase of inventory
   (h) Carriage on inventory
   (i) Legal costs in buying new business
   (j) Repayment of loan
   (k) New computer network installation costs
   (l) Commission received

## Practice

**4** A new heating system is installed in a business office. The costs of this system in its first year are shown below.

| | $ |
|---|---|
| Purchase price of boiler | 1870 |
| Purchase price of pipework | 280 |
| Annual servicing costs of system | 190 |
| Gas bill associated with the heating system | 485 |
| Repair costs | 224 |
| Delivery charge of boiler and pipework | 55 |

Calculate the amounts to be included in capital and revenue expenditure.

**5** A business purchases a second-hand van for business use. The purchase price is $3000 but there are additional costs associated with the purchase. The van needs new tyres to make it safe – the current tyres are dangerous and prevent the van from being used. The tyres cost $575 for four. Tax on the van – a yearly cost – is $350. Fuel costs for the year are estimated to be $4780. The business logo is painted on the side of the van at a cost of $520.

The capital expenditure associated with the purchase of the van the statement of financial position as the value of the van. Calculate the value of the van recorded on the statement of financial position.

**6** The following costs relate to the running of a fast-food shop that specialises in pizza. Decide whether the costs are capital or revenue expenditure, and calculate the total for each category.

| | $ |
|---|---|
| (a) Purchase of food ingredients | 3145 |
| (b) Cost of installing a new cooker | 900 |
| (c) Wages paid to shop staff | 14141 |
| (d) Insurance of premises | 2378 |
| (e) Cost of delivery of drinks to be sold | 188 |
| (f) Cost of advertising | 444 |
| (g) Legal costs of expanding premises | 1560 |
| (h) Cost of boxes used for pizzas | 490 |
| (i) New sign outside shop | 2990 |

## Stretch

**7** The following draft profit for a year contains a number of errors due to incorrect classification of capital and revenue expenditures and receipts. In addition, the figure for gross profit includes $550 which was earned on the sale of assets used in the business.

**(a)** Prepare a corrected statement of profit for the year.

**(b)** Use the corrected profit for the year to calculate the change in the profit.

**(c)** Calculate the change to the value of the business's assets.

| | $ | $ |
|---|---|---|
| Gross profit | | 16 250 |
| Add: Bank loan | 5 000 | |
| Add: Rent received | 2 310 | 7 310 |
| | | 23 560 |
| Less expenses: | | |
| Insurance | 875 | |
| Wages | 12 500 | |
| Transport of goods to customers | 260 | |
| Office furniture | 1 890 | |
| Marketing costs | 450 | |
| Owner's drawings | 3 000 | |
| Delivery cost of office furniture | 345 | 19 320 |
| Profit for the year | | 4 240 |

## Unit review

1 Which of the following would be included as capital expenditure?

   **A** Repairing window frames

   **B** Fixing a leak to the heating system

   **C** Installation of solar panels on the roof

   **D** Plastering minor areas of old walls

2 Which of the following would not count as revenue expenditure for a bakery?

   **A** Purchase of flour

   **B** Purchase of new ovens

   **C** Delivery cost of new vans for deliveries

   **D** Wages paid to bakers

3 Which of the following is treated as a capital receipt by a decorator?

   **A** Income received for painting a large building

   **B** Purchase of new paint

   **C** Sale of old van used in business

   **D** Income received for selling unwanted paint

4 What is the effect of including revenue expenditure within capital expenditure?

   **A** Reported profits are higher

   **B** Assets are undervalued

   **C** Reported profits are lower

   **D** Liabilities are overvalued

# 4.2 Accounting for depreciation and disposal of non-current assets

## Check your progress

| Read the unit objectives below. Tick the column that best describes your progress in each. | ▲ | ▲▲ | ▲▲▲ |
|---|---|---|---|
| define depreciation | | | |
| explain the reasons for accounting for depreciation | | | |
| name and describe the straight line, reducing balance and revaluation methods of depreciation | | | |
| prepare ledger accounts and journal entries for the provision of depreciation | | | |
| prepare ledger accounts and journal entries to record the sale of non-current assets, including the use of disposal accounts. | | | |

## Support

1 A machine is purchased for $80 000. It is expected to last five years and have no residual value. It is depreciated using the straight line method. Calculate the depreciation each year.

2 Equipment is purchased for $100 000. It is depreciated using the reducing balance method at a rate of 20%. Calculate the depreciation for the first two years of the equipment's life.

3 Fixtures and fittings are sold for $6700. The fixtures originally cost $12 000 and had been depreciated by $6000 by the date of sale. Calculate the profit or loss on the disposal of this asset.

## Practice

4 Equipment is purchased for $25 000. It is expected to last for four years with a residual value of $5000. It is depreciated using the straight line method. Calculate the yearly depreciation and the net book value at the end of the first two years of the equipment's life.

5 New office fixtures are purchased for $60 000 with a useful life of 10 years. The fixtures have no residual value. Calculate the depreciation and net book values for years 1–5 using the straight line method and reducing balance method of depreciation. Use a rate of 10% when using the reducing balance method.

6 A van costing $48 000 is purchased for business use on 1 January 2018. It is depreciated using the reducing balance method at a rate of 25%. Prepare the provision for depreciation account for the van for the first three years of its life. (The business year ends on 31 December.)

7 Machinery is sold for $5000. The machinery originally cost $42 000 and had been depreciated using the straight line method based on an expected life of eight years and no residual value. The machinery was sold seven years after its purchase. Prepare the disposal account and the entries in the general journal relating to the sale of the machinery. Narratives are required.

## Stretch

**8**   A business purchases the following equipment.

Equipment A    1 January 2018    $20000
Equipment B    30 April 2018    $12000
Equipment C    30 June 2018    $40000
Equipment D    1 October 2018    $20000

The straight line method of depreciation is used. Depreciation is provided for fractions of a year. The machinery is assumed to last five years with no residual value. On 30 June 2019, Equipment B is sold for $8300.

(a) Prepare ledger accounts as follows:

(i)  Equipment for the year ended 31 December 2018

(ii)  Provision for depreciation of equipment for the year ended 31 December 2018

(iii)  Equipment disposal for the year ended 31 December 2019.

(b) Prepare the entries in the general journal to record the disposal of Equipment B. Narratives are not required.

## Unit review

**1**   Which of the following is not a recognised method of depreciation?

A  Straight line method

B  Reducing balance method

C  Revaluation method

D  Disposal method

**2**   Fixtures are bought for business use for $7500. They are depreciated using the straight line method. They are expected to last 10 years with a residual value of $500. What is the net book value of the fixtures after five years?

A  $4000

B  $3500

C  $3750

D  $4250

**3**   Computers are purchased for $8000 and are depreciated using the reducing balance method at a rate of 25%. What is the depreciation to be provided for in year 2 of the computers' life?

A  $2000

B  $1500

C  $2500

D  $3000

**4**   Equipment is bought for $15000 and is depreciated using the reducing balance method at 20%. It is sold for $4000 after two years of use. What is the profit or loss on the equipment's disposal?

A  Loss of $8000

B  Loss of $5000

C  Loss of $5600

D  Loss of $4400

# 4.3 Other payables and other receivables

## Check your progress

| Read the unit objectives below. Tick the column that best describes your progress in each. | ▲ | ▲▲ | ▲▲ |
|---|---|---|---|
| recognise the importance of matching costs and revenues | | | |
| prepare ledger accounts and journal entries to record accrued and prepaid expenses | | | |
| prepare ledger accounts and journal entries to record accrued and prepaid incomes. | | | |

## Support

1   For each of the following items, calculate the amount to be included in the income statement.

   (a) Rent paid in 2018: $4900; Owing at 31 December 2018: $55

   (b) Insurance paid in 2018: $880; prepaid for 2019: $150

   (c) Wages paid in 2018: $22000; owing at year end: $650

2   For each of the following items, calculate the amount to be included in the income statement.

   (a) Rent received in 2018: $9500; still owed to business at year end: $560

   (b) Commission received in 2018: $760; received in 2018 for 2019: $35

   (c) Royalties received in 2018: $450; received in 2018 for 2017: $80

## Practice

3   The following transactions took place in the financial year ended 31 December 2018. Prepare a ledger account and entries in the general journal for each of the following.

   (a) Heating and lighting paid during 2018 totalled $985, but as at 31 December 2018 there was $76 still owing.

   (b) Rent paid during 2018 totalled $8900. Out of the total paid, $775 was for January 2019.

4   The following transactions took place during the financial year ended 31 December 2018. Prepare a ledger account and entries in the general journal for each of the following.

   (a) Insurance paid in 2018 was $1010, including $99 for 2019.

   (b) Payments received for commission during the year totalled $2090. At the end of the year the business is still owed $230.

5   A business's electricity expenses are paid in 2018 as follows.

| Date payment made | Amount paid | Period payment made for |
|---|---|---|
| 4 Jan | $500 | 1 Jan – 31 May |
| 29 May | $500 | 1 Jun – 31 Oct |
| 18 Nov | $500 | 1 Nov – 31 Mar |

Prepare a ledger account for the electricity expense for the year ended 31 December 2018.

**6**  The following are the amounts paid and received for the year ended 31 December 2018.
For each item, calculate the amounts to be deducted from or added to the profit for the year.

| Items paid and received | Amounts paid | Amounts received |
|---|---|---|
| Wages | $22 300 | |
| Commission received | | $4 500 |
| Gas and electricity | $3 670 | |

| | Additional information | |
|---|---|---|
| | As at 31 Dec 2017 | As at 31 Dec 2018 |
| Wages | Balance owing $450 | Balance owing $910 |
| Commission received | Balance owing $86 | Balance prepaid $113 |
| Gas and electricity | Balance prepaid $199 | Balance owing $87 |

## Stretch

**7**  Prepare the ledger accounts for the following items.

(a) General expenses owing as at 1 January 2018: $44; amounts paid during 2018: $754 general expenses owing as at 31 December 2018: $81

(b) Marketing costs owing as at 1 Jan 2018: $55; amounts paid during 2018: $1243; marketing costs prepaid as at 31 December 2018: $22

(c) Insurance paid in advance in 2017 for the year 2018: $310; insurance paid during 2018: $4190; insurance owing as at 31 December 2018: $410

(d) Rent received during 2018: $2840; amount owing to the business as at 1 January 2018: $387; amount owing to the business as at 31 December 2018: $118

## Unit review

**1**  What is an amount received by a business in advance of the period it is due known as?

A  Accrued expense      C  Accrued income

B  Prepaid expense      D  Prepaid income

**2**  Which of the following appears as a balance brought down on the credit side in a ledger account at the start of an accounting period?

A  Expenses paid in advance      C  Accrued expenses

B  Prepaid expenses      D  Accrued income

**3**  At the start of the year a business owed $45 for rent. At the end of the year it owed $67. Rent paid during the year is $3800. How much will appear in the income statement for rent?

A  $3800      C  $3822

B  $3912      D  $3778

**4**  Royalties received in advance at the start of the year total $12. During the year amounts received for royalties total $466. At the end of the year royalties received in advance of the next year total $91. How much income should be credited to the current year's income statement for royalties?

A  $387      C  $466

B  $545      D  $363

# 4.4 Irrecoverable debts and provision for doubtful debts

## Check your progress

| Read the unit objectives below. Tick the column that best describes your progress in each. | ▲ | ▲▲ | ▲▲▲ |
|---|---|---|---|
| understand the meaning of irrecoverable debts and recovery of debts written off | | | |
| prepare ledger accounts and journal entries to record irrecoverable debts | | | |
| prepare ledger accounts and journal entries to record recovery of debts written off | | | |
| explain the reasons for maintaining a provision for doubtful debts | | | |
| prepare ledger accounts and journal entries to record the creation of, and adjustments to, a provision for doubtful debts. | | | |

## Support

1   During 2018 a business decides to write off the following debts as irrecoverable.

   31 Mar    Adebisi    $89

   27 June    Pedro    $190

   Prepare the irrecoverable debts account for the year.

2   The provision for doubtful debts at the start of the year is $820. Trade receivables at the year end are $20000. The business maintains the provision for doubtful debts at 5% of trade receivables. Calculate the amount entered in the year's income statement for provision for doubtful debts.

## Practice

3   A new business started trading on 1 January 2018 and the following debts are written off as irrecoverable during the year.

   26 July    Ariel    $75

   31 Aug    Luiz    $81

   8 Nov    Javiera    $24

   Prepare the irrecoverable debts account for 2018.

4   Yuuma is a credit customer who owes a business $960. He is declared bankrupt. Most of the debt is deemed irrecoverable. However, after the sale of the business assets of the customer the business received $0.25 for every $1 owed. This is in full settlement of the outstanding amount. Prepare the account of Yuuma after all the transactions have occurred.

5   Denys increases the current provision for doubtful debts from $450 to $620 for the financial year ending 31 December 2018. Prepare the provision for doubtful debts account for the full year and the entries in the general journal to record this transaction.

**6** A debt written off in 2017 as irrecoverable is recovered when full settlement is received on 23 February 2018. The original debt totalled $317 and was owed by Benet. Prepare the account of Benet and the irrecoverable debts recovered account for the year ending 31 December 2018.

## Stretch

**7** A new business decides at the end of the first year to create a provision for doubtful debts. For 2018/19, the provision is maintained at 4% of the year-end value for trade receivables. Due to a worsening economic outlook, the provision is increased to 5% of trade receivables for 2020/1.

Use the following data to prepare the provision for doubtful debts account for the years ending 31 December 2018–21 and the entries in the general journal to record these adjustments. Narratives are not required.

| Trade receivables at year end | |
|---|---|
| | **$** |
| 2018 | 18 500 |
| 2019 | 21 000 |
| 2020 | 23 000 |
| 2021 | 20 500 |

## Unit review

**1** Which of the following factors is the most likely explanation for why a business has increased its provision for doubtful debts?

**A** Credit customers repaying in shorter periods

**B** Economic outlook improving

**C** Lower risks of business failure

**D** Business moving into industry characterised by poor payment of debts

**2** Which of the following is debited to the income statement?

**A** Irrecoverable debts

**B** Decreases in the provision for doubtful debts

**C** Maintenance of the same size for the provision for doubtful debts

**D** Recovery of debts written off

**3** A business changes its provision for doubtful debts from $890 to $680. What entry is made in the income statement to record this change?

**A** Debit entry of $210          **C** Debit entry of $680

**B** Credit entry of $210          **D** Credit entry of $890

**4** Which of the following is the best description of how trade receivables appear on the statement of financial position?

**A** In full with no deductions

**B** With only irrecoverable debts subtracted

**C** With the full provision for doubtful debts subtracted

**D** With the change in the provision for doubtful debts subtracted

# 4.5 Valuation of inventory

## Check your progress

| Read the unit objectives below. Tick the column that best describes your progress in each. | ▲ | ▲▲ | ▲▲ |
|---|---|---|---|
| understand the basis of the valuation of inventory at the lower of cost and net realisable value | | | |
| prepare simple inventory valuation statements | | | |
| recognise the importance of valuation of inventory and the effect of an incorrect valuation of inventory on gross profit, profit for the year, equity, and asset valuation. | | | |

## Support

1   Select from the following words to complete the gaps in the sentence below. Not all words will be used.

price, realisable, lowest, highest, replacement, cost

Inventory should be valued at selling _____ or net _____ value, whichever is _____.

2   Inventory cost $43. It can now be sold for $39. On the statement of financial position, what is the correct value of this inventory?

3   A business buys 90 units of inventory for $5 each. After a fire in the business warehouse the inventory is damaged and can now be sold as a whole batch for $490. The inventory needs repair for the fire damage and this will cost $100.

(a)  For the whole batch, what is the cost value of the inventory?

(b)  For the whole batch, what is the net realisable value of the inventory?

(c)  What is the correct value for the inventory in the accounts?

(i) $450

(ii) $390

(iii) $390

4   Select from the following words to complete the gaps in the sentence below. Not all words will be used.

unaffected, overvalued, undervalued

If inventory is undervalued then assets on the financial statement are _____ and profits for the year are _____

## Practice

5   Inventory cost $48. It is damaged and can now be sold for $60 if $13 is spent on repairing the inventory. What is the correct value of this inventory?

6   A business purchased 15 units of inventory for $11 each. The inventory is damaged. The whole batch of inventory can now be sold for $180, but this requires spending $40 on repairing the inventory. How much should the inventory be valued at in the accounts?

**7** Look at the following inventory valuation statement. Calculate the value of closing inventory as at 31 July 2018.

| Inventory valuation statement as at 31 July 2018 | | | | |
|---|---|---|---|---|
| | No. of items held | Original CPU ($) | NRV ($) | Total value |
| Product X | 8 | 6 | 5 | |
| Product Y | 12 | 8 | 9 | |
| Product Z | 20 | 11 | 14 | |
| Total value of inventory held | | | | |

## Stretch

**8** Closing inventory cost $27 000. The closing inventory is damaged and could be sold for $30 000 if $5000 is spent on repairs. The business values inventory at cost. Calculate the effect on profit for the year if the inventory is valued correctly.

**9** Kandeel has purchased six batches of electrical parts – shown by their component reference in the table below. Each batch is damaged and will cost money to repair. Kandeel has valued all the components on his balance sheet at cost value.

| Component reference | Cost per item $ | Selling price per item $ | Repair cost for whole batch $ | Number of components in batch |
|---|---|---|---|---|
| AK3 | 4 | 8 | 18 | 12 |
| KE4 | 6 | 9 | 80 | 15 |
| MA8 | 11 | 16 | 90 | 20 |
| EB33 | 19 | 25 | 22 | 4 |
| BN18 | 13 | 19 | 64 | 14 |

(a) Calculate the correct value of the total batches for Kandeel.

(b) State how the balance sheet value of assets will change as a result of any changes to the valuation of the components.

(c) Explain how equity is affected by this change in inventory valuation.

## Unit review

**1** What is the correct value for the following inventory?

80 units were purchased for $3 each. The whole batch is damaged and can be sold for only $250. If repair work is done, the batch could be sold for $300. The repair work will cost $45.

A $240          B $300          C $255          D $250

**2** If closing inventory is undervalued, which of the following is true?

A Assets are overvalued          C Revenue is undervalued

B Profits are overvalued          D Assets are undervalued

**3** Which of the following is the correct method for valuing inventory?

A Always at cost

B At cost or selling price whichever is highest

C Replacement cost or net realisable value whichever is lowest

D Lowest of cost or net realisable value

# Chapter 4 review

**1** Which of the following is not a capital receipt?

    **A** Bank loan obtained                 **C** Commission received

    **B** Owner's equity contribution of money    **D** Selling price of non-current asset

**2** Revenue expenditure is mistakenly classed as capital expenditure. Which of the following is true?

    **A** Profits are understated               **C** Asset valuations are overstated

    **B** Profits are unaffected                **D** Asset valuations are unaffected

**3** A business depreciates its assets using the straight line method. Which of the following pieces of information is not required to calculate depreciation?

    **A** Original cost of asset                **C** Expected useful life

    **B** Reason(s) for loss in value of asset      **D** Any residual value

**4** A machine cost $48 000 and is depreciated using the reducing balance method at a rate of 25%. What is the net book value of the machine after two years of ownership?

    **A** $24 000          **B** $36 000             **C** $27 000             **D** $12 000

**5** A car has a net book value of $5500 and is sold for $6800. How is profit for the business affected by this sale?

    **A** Increased by $1300               **C** Increased by $6800

    **B** Decreased by $1300              **D** Decreased by $5500

**6** Equipment is purchased for $28 000 and is expected to last for 10 years. The expected residual value is $3000. What is the net book value of the equipment after three years?

    **A** $23 000          **B** $25 000             **C** $19 600             **D** $20 500

**7** Rent owing to a business at the year-end is best described as which of the following?

    **A** Prepaid expense                 **C** Accrued expense

    **B** Accrued revenue                 **D** Prepaid revenue

**8** Business rates are $400 per month. Prepaid business rates were $450 at the start of the year and $500 was owing at the end of the year. How much did the business pay for business rates during the year?

    **A** $4800            **B** $3850              **C** $4750              **D** $3950

**9** A business has 18 units of inventory costing $16 per unit. A fire damages this inventory. Only 10 units remain suitable for sale for $20 each. However, $35 needs to be spent on getting these units ready for sale. How much should the 10 units be valued at in the accounts?

    **A** $160             **B** $200               **C** $125               **D** $355

**10** Closing inventory is overvalued. Which of the following is correct?

| | Effect on profits | Effect on asset valuations |
|---|---|---|
| **A** | Overvalued | Overvalued |
| **B** | Overvalued | Undervalued |
| **C** | Undervalued | Overvalued |
| **D** | Undervalued | Undervalued |

11 Hashim is a trader. His financial year ends on 31 December. He maintains a combined account for gas and electricity costs.

On 1 January 2018, he owed $43 for gas costs for 2017. He also had two months electricity paid in advance for 2018 totalling $350. The monthly costs for each are as follows.

   Gas $150; Electricity $175

During the year ended 31 December 2018, Hashim made the following payments by cheque.

   Gas $1650; Electricity $1980

Hashim receives commission for additional work undertaken. In 2017 he received a cheque for $75 for commission on work due to be completed in 2018.

During 2018 he received the following cheques.

   7 August 2018          $340

   11 September 2018      $560

As at 31 December 2018, he is still owed commission of $55. He is unsure if this amount will be collected. He is advised to write to the customer to find out when the money will be received.

(a) Prepare the combined account for gas and electricity costs for the year ended 31 December 2018. Balance the account and bring down the balances to 1 January 2019.    [8]

(b) State in which section of the statement of financial position the outstanding balance for electricity as at 31 December 2018 appears. Give a reason for your answer.    [2]

(c) Prepare the commission received account for the year ended 31 December 2018. Balance the account and bring down the balance to 1 January 2019.    [5]

(d) Give three reasons why a business may experience an increase in irrecoverable debts.    [3]

(e) Hashim decides that the commission owing is to be written off as uncollectable. State the accounts to be debited and credited.    [2]

[Total 20]

12 Didi runs her business from her home office. The following balances were extracted from her books on 30 April 2018.

|  | $ |
| --- | --- |
| Inventory as at 1 May 2018 | 5245 |
| Revenue (sales) | 79656 |
| Purchases | 42511 |
| Recovery of debts written off | 213 |
| Irrecoverable debts | 545 |
| Provision for doubtful debts | 660 |
| Provision for depreciation of machinery | 8750 |
| Machinery | 25900 |
| Trade receivables | 7555 |
| Trade payables | 2432 |
| Wages | 11212 |
| General expenses | 8785 |
| Owner's equity | ? |

(a) Prepare Didi's trial balance as at 30 April 2018 showing the balance on the owner's equity account. [14]

(b) The machinery is depreciated using the reducing balance method at a rate of 20%. Calculate the value of depreciation on the machinery for the year ended 30 April 2018. [2]

(c) State the ledger in which the provision for depreciation of machinery account appears. [1]

(d) All the machinery is sold for $11 000 on 1 May 2018. No depreciation is provided for after the end of the year to 30 April 2018. Calculate the profit or loss on the disposal of the machinery. [2]

(e) State the book of prime entry in which depreciation is recorded? [1]

[Total 20]

13 Lawson is a trader. His business year ends on 31 March. The following is a trial balance extract from the most recent year-end.

| Lawson | | |
|---|---|---|
| Trial balance extract as at 31 March 2018 | | |
| | Dr ($) | Cr ($) |
| Trade receivables | 8750 | |
| Provision for doubtful debts | | 248 |
| Equipment at cost | 26500 | |
| Provision for depreciation of equipment | | 12800 |

Lawson realises he has failed to account for the following items.

(i) Matheus – a credit customer – has recently ceased trading. He owes Lawson $300. Lawson is to write this off as an irrecoverable debt.

(ii) The provision for doubtful debts is to be maintained at 4% of trade receivables. The trial balance total has not been adjusted for the irrecoverable debt.

(iii) Deprecation on equipment is to be provided at 15% using the reducing balance method.

(iv) A debt written off as irrecoverable – valued at $120 – from Lotte was received in full during the financial year.

(a) Profit for the year was originally calculated at $9900. Calculate the corrected profit after taking into account the items above. [7]

(b) Prepare the general journal entries to record items (i)–(iii). Narratives are not required. [6]

(c) State the book of prime entry in which item (iv) is recorded. [1]

(d) State whether each of the following items should be recorded as capital expenditure or revenue expenditure. [6]

(i) Purchase of business premises

(ii) Repairs to brickwork

(iii) Purchase of office furniture

(iv) Transport costs of office furniture to business

(v) Wage costs

(vi) Depreciation on office furniture

[Total 20]

# 5 Preparation of financial statements

## 5.1 Sole traders

### Check your progress

| Read the unit objectives below. Tick the column that best describes your progress in each. | ▲ | ▲▲ | ▲▲▲ |
|---|---|---|---|
| explain the advantages and disadvantages of operating as a sole trader | | | |
| explain the importance of preparing income statements and statements of financial position | | | |
| explain the difference between a trading business and a service business | | | |
| prepare income statements for trading businesses and for service businesses | | | |
| understand that statements of financial position record assets and liabilities on a specified date | | | |
| recognise and define the content of a statement of financial position: non-current assets, intangible assets, current assets, current liabilities, non-current liabilities and capital | | | |
| understand the interrelationship of items in a statement of financial position | | | |
| prepare statements of financial position for trading businesses and service businesses | | | |
| make adjustments for provision for depreciation using the straight line, reducing balance and revaluation methods | | | |
| make adjustments for accrued and prepaid expenses and accrued and prepaid income | | | |
| make adjustments for irrecoverable debts and provisions for doubtful debts | | | |
| make adjustments for goods taken by the owner for own use. | | | |

### Support

1   Explain what is meant by 'unlimited liability'.

2   Abid runs a fabric store operating as a sole trader. He has provided the following information for the year ended 30 April 2018.

Prepare Abid's trading account for the year ended 30 April 2018.

| | $ |
|---|---|
| Revenue | 45663 |
| Purchases | 29361 |
| Inventory as at 1 May 2017 | 15723 |
| Inventory as at 30 April 2018 | 4077 |
| Sales returns | 2300 |
| Purchases returns | 1089 |
| Carriage inwards | 1563 |
| Carriage outwards | 2623 |

3   Bina is a sole trader who runs a business that sells sandwiches to local businesses. She has extracted the following information from her books of account for the year ended 31 January 2018.

| | $ |
|---|---|
| Revenue | 25582 |
| Purchases | 7980 |
| Inventory as at 1 February 2017 | 325 |
| Inventory as at 31 January 2018 | 153 |
| Wages and salaries | 7850 |
| Delivery expenses | 3150 |
| Rent | 2130 |
| Insurance | 320 |
| General expenses | 290 |

Prepare Bina's income statement for the year ended 31 January 2018.

## Practice

4   Luna is a sole trader who runs BFC book store. She has extracted the following information from her books of account for the year ended 30 April 2018.

| | $ |
|---|---|
| Sales | 170000 |
| Purchases | 50000 |
| Opening Inventory | 20000 |
| Closing Inventory | 10000 |

Calculate BFC book store's cost of sales and gross profit.

5   Hasan operates as a sole trader selling luxury cruises. He has extracted the following information from his books of account for the year ended 31 May 2018.

| | $ |
|---|---|
| Commission received | 39500 |
| Administration expenses | 10700 |
| Office rent | 7514 |
| Office equipment cost | 30000 |
| Stationery and printing costs | 3940 |
| Insurance | 1900 |
| General expenses | 3900 |
| Office equipment depreciation | 6000 |

**Additional Information**

On 31 May 2018:

- Insurance had been prepaid: $300
- Commission received earned but unpaid: $2055
- Depreciation is to be charged on the office equipment at 20% per annum on cost

Prepare Hasan's income statement for the year ended 31 May 2018.

6    Jayne is a self-employed baker who own Dolphins bakery. She has prepared the following trial balance from her books of account on 30 April 2018.

| Dolphins bakery Trial balance as at 30 April 2018 | Dr | Cr |
|---|---|---|
| | $ | $ |
| Revenue | | 57588 |
| Purchases | 47606 | |
| Office expenses | 1708 | |
| Lighting and heating expenses | 844 | |
| Salaries and wages | 6328 | |
| Insurance | 210 | |
| Buildings | 103012 | |
| Trade receivables | 6332 | |
| Trade payables | | 2192 |
| Bank | 4694 | |
| Inventory: 1 May 2017 | 3000 | |
| Drawings | 5700 | |
| Delivery vehicles | 10100 | |
| Provision for depreciation: delivery vehicles | | 2020 |
| Delivery vehicle expenses | 2266 | |
| Capital | | 130000 |
| | 191800 | 191800 |

**Additional information**

On 30 April 2018:

- Lighting and heating expenses prepaid: $250
- Motor vehicle expenses due but unpaid: $500
- Inventory on 30 April 2018: $18000
- Depreciation is to be charged on the delivery vehicle at 20% on cost

Prepare the income statement for Dolphins bakery for the year ended 30 April 2018 and the statement of financial position as at 30 April 2018.

## Stretch

7   Aadi has provided the following list of balances from his books of account as at 31 March 2018.

| | $ |
|---|---|
| Motor vehicle | 23 500 |
| Office equipment | 15 750 |
| Inventory | 3 500 |
| Cash at bank | 2 500 |
| Trade receivables | 5 000 |
| Trade payables | 3 000 |
| Bank overdraft | 1 500 |
| Drawings | 9 500 |
| Capital | ? |

Calculate the value of Aadi's capital.

8   Discuss how a sole trader's annual financial statements may allow the owner to assess the profitability and liquidity of their business.

## Unit review

1   Which of the following is classified as an intangible non-current asset?

A  Buildings          B  Cash at bank          C  Goodwill          D  Motor car

2   Which of the following is used to calculate a business's cost of sales?

(a)  Closing inventory          (c)  Purchases
(b)  Opening inventory          (d)  Revenue

A  (a), (b) and (c)          C  (a), (b), (c) and (d)
B  (a), (c) and (d)          D  (b), (c) and (d)

3   Which of the following appear in an income statement and a statement of financial position?

A  Gross profit          C  Profit for the year
B  Opening inventory          D  Total expenses

4   The purchase of office equipment has been debited in error to the purchases account.
What is the effect of this error on the financial statements?

| | Profit for the year | | Non-current asset total | |
|---|---|---|---|---|
| | Too high | Too low | Too high | Too low |
| A | ✓ | | ✓ | |
| B | ✓ | | | ✓ |
| C | | ✓ | ✓ | |
| D | | ✓ | | ✓ |

# 5.2 Partnerships

## Check your progress

| Read the unit objectives below. Tick the column that best describes your progress in each. | ▲ | ▲▲ | ▲▲ |
|---|---|---|---|
| explain the advantages and disadvantages of forming a partnership | | | |
| outline the importance and contents of a partnership agreement | | | |
| explain the purpose of an appropriation account | | | |
| prepare income statements, appropriation accounts and statements of financial position | | | |
| record interest on partners' loans, interest on capital, interest on drawings, partners' salaries and the division of the balance of profit or loss | | | |
| make adjustments to financial statements as detailed in 5.1 (sole traders) | | | |
| explain the uses of, and differences between, capital and current accounts | | | |
| draw up partners' capital and current accounts in ledger account form and as part of a statement of financial position. | | | |

## Support

1   Explain what is meant by a deed of partnership.

2   Explain the difference between a capital account and a current account.

3   Alfredo, Giovanni and Katya are in partnership. Their partnership agreement states the following.

   1   Profits and losses will be shared in the ratio of 3 : 2 : 1.
   2   Interest on capital is allowed at 10% per annum.
   3   Alfredo will receive a partnership salary of $10 000 per annum.
   4   Interest on drawings is charged at 5% on balances at the end of the year.

   As at 31 December 2018, the following balances were extracted from the books of account.

| | $ |
|---|---|
| Profit for the year | 63 000 |
| Capital account balances: | |
|    Alfredo | 32 000 |
|    Giovanni | 24 000 |
|    Katya | 24 000 |
| Drawings: | |
|    Alfredo | 18 000 |
|    Giovanni | 12 000 |
|    Katya | 12 000 |

   Prepare the appropriation account for Alfredo, Giovanni and Katya for the year ended 31 December 2018.

## Practice

**4** Amir and Harman are in partnership. Their partnership agreement contains the following.

- Profits and losses are shared in the ratio of 2 : 1
- Interest is allowed on capital at 5%
- Amir will receive a partnership salary of $12000.

Interest on drawings will be charged at a rate of 4% on balances at the end of the year.

As at 31 December 2018, the following balances were extracted from the books of account:

| | $ |
|---|---|
| Profit for the year | 40000 |
| Current account balances: | |
| Amir | 8100 |
| Harman | 9320 |
| Capital account balances: | |
| Amir | 30000 |
| Harman | 20000 |
| Drawings: | |
| Amir | 18200 |
| Harman | 13750 |

Prepare the appropriation account for Amir and Harman for the year ended 31 December 2018 and the current account for both partners for the same period.

**5** Xi, Yorath and Zane are in partnership. Their financial year ends on 31 October 2018. They have provided the following information from their books of account.

| | Xi | Yorath | Zane |
|---|---|---|---|
| | $ | $ | $ |
| On 1 November 2017: | | | |
| Capital account | 100000 | 140000 | 180000 |
| Current account | 390 Cr | 1860 Dr | 1540 Cr |
| On 31 October 2018: | | | |
| Drawings | 30000 | 22000 | 34000 |
| Interest on drawings | 900 | 660 | 1020 |
| Interest on capital | 10000 | 14000 | 18000 |
| Partner's salaries | | 19000 | |
| Profit share | 50000 | 100000 | 150000 |

Prepare the capital accounts and current accounts for all three partners and show the capital section of their balance sheet as at 31 October 2018.

## Stretch

**6** Benjamin and Melinda are planning to work in partnership as travel agents. Ben has more experience than Melinda in this role, but Melinda is willing to provide more capital to start up the business. Advise Benjamin and Melinda what they should include in their deed of partnership prior to opening the business.

**7** Discuss the relevance of a debit balance on a partner's current balance.

# Unit review

1   Which of the following appear in an income statement but not in the appropriation account of a partnership?

   **(a)** Drawings                                    **(c)** Interest on loans
   **(b)** Interest on drawings                         **(d)** Purchases

   **A** (a), (b) and (c)        **B** (a), (c) and (d)        **C** (b), (c) and (d)        **D** (a), (b), (c) and (d)

2   A partnership's financial year ends on 31 October 2018. On 1 August 2018, $9000 was paid for rent for the six months to 31 December 2018. What is the correct entry in the statement of financial position on 30 September 2018?

   **A** Accrual $4500                                  **C** Prepayment $4500
   **B** Accrual $000                                   **D** Prepayment $000

3   In a set of partnership accounts, an irrecoverable debt has been omitted. What is the effect of this omission?

   **A** Current liabilities overstated                **C** Profit for the year overstated
   **B** Current liabilities understated               **D** Profit for the year understated

4   Which of the following are classified as a current asset within a partnership business?

   **(a)** Cash at bank                                 **(c)** Prepaid account for electricity
   **(b)** Money owed by a customer                     **(d)** Unpaid invoice from a supplier

   **A** (a), (b) and (c)        **B** (a), (c) and (d)        **C** (a), (b), (c) and (d)        **D** (b), (c) and (d)

# 5.3 Limited companies

## Check your progress

| Read the unit objectives below. Tick the column that best describes your progress in each. | ▲ | ▲▲ | ▲▲▲ |
|---|---|---|---|
| explain the advantages and disadvantages of operating as a limited company | | | |
| understand the meaning of the term limited liability | | | |
| understand the meaning of the term equity | | | |
| understand the capital structure of a limited company comprising preference share capital, ordinary share capital, general reserve and retained earnings | | | |
| understand and distinguish between issued, called-up and paid-up share capital | | | |
| understand and distinguish between share capital (preference shares and ordinary shares) and loan capital (debentures) | | | |
| prepare income statements, statements of changes in equity and statements of financial position | | | |
| make adjustments to financial statements as detailed in Unit 5.1 (sole traders). | | | |

## Support

1   The following relates to the capital of Nettleship plc.

- Authorised share capital: 100 000 000 $1 ordinary shares
- Issued share capital: 700 000 $1 ordinary shares

A dividend of $0.055 per share is paid. Calculate the value of this dividend.

2   The following relates to the capital of Boaler plc.

Issued share capital:

- 500 000 $1 ordinary shares
- 220 000 4% $1 preference shares

In addition to the preference dividend, a dividend of $0.02 per share is paid in full. Calculate the total dividend paid by Boaler plc.

# Practice

3 Bruno Limited was formed by three sisters on 1 April 2017. The company produced a Memorandum of Association that stated it could issue 500000 shares of $1.50 each. The company decided to offer 350000 shares for sale at $1.50 each. The terms of the issue were:

- 50% of the amount due was to be paid immediately
- 50% was to be paid on 1 November 2017.

On 1 October 2017, the holders of 200000 shares had paid the amount due.

State:

(a) the authorised share capital on 1 October 2017

(b) the issued share capital on 1 October 2017

(c) the called-up share capital on 1 October 2017

(d) the paid-up share capital on 1 October 2017.

4 The following trial balance was prepared by Atom Enterprises Ltd as at 31 December 2018.

| Atom Enterprises Ltd Trial balance as at 31 December 2018 | | |
|---|---|---|
| | $ | $ |
| $1 ordinary shares | | 100000 |
| 5% $1 preference shares | | 30000 |
| Retained earnings | | 20000 |
| Non-current assets | 195000 | |
| Revenue | | 210500 |
| Purchases | 130000 | |
| Opening inventory | 17800 | |
| Distribution costs | 11500 | |
| Administration costs | 8800 | |
| Directors remuneration | 6750 | |
| Trade receivables and payables | 16900 | 10950 |
| Cash and cash equivalents | 25700 | |
| Provision for depreciation on non-current assets | | 4500 |
| 6% debentures | | 40000 |
| Share premium account | | |
| Ordinary dividend paid | 2000 | |
| Preference dividend paid | 1500 | |
| | 415950 | 415950 |

## Additional information

1 Depreciation is to be provided on non-current assets at 20% using reducing balance

2 Inventory as at 31 December 2017 was $34500

3 Finance costs due but unpaid for the year totalled $3400

4 A transfer was made to the general reserve of $5000

5 The debenture interest is accrued as at 31 December 2018.

Prepare an income statement for the year ended 31 December 2018 and a balance sheet as at that date.

## Stretch

**5** Weishuan owns two juice bars. These are both located near a large university in a big city. The juice bars are very successful and she wishes to expand. Currently the business is operated as a private limited company. Weishuan is considering turning the business into a public limited company. Advise her on this issue.

**6** Why would an investor buy shares in a company that had a policy of not giving out dividends to shareholders?

**7** Why do you think a company would issue shares at a premium?

## Unit review

**1** In which section of a company's statement of financial position would an item of capital expenditure appear?

**A** Current assets        **C** Non-current assets

**B** Current liabilities       **D** Non-current liabilities

**2** Shares which remain in existence indefinitely and are classified as equity in the statement of financial position are known as:

**A** Redeemable ordinary shares

**B** Non-redeemable ordinary shares

**C** Redeemable preference shares

**D** Non-redeemable preference shares

**3** The maximum amount of share capital that can be issued by a limited company is known as:

**A** Authorised share capital      **C** Issued share capital

**B** Called-up share capital       **D** Paid-up share capital

**4** LJO Limited has the following capital structure:

- 1 000 000 ordinary shares of $6 each
- Shareholders will receive a dividend of 5%

What is the total amount LJO Limited will pay in dividends?

**A** $200 000          **B** $250 000          **C** $300 000          **D** $350 000

# 5.4 Clubs and societies

## Check your progress

| Read the unit objectives below. Tick the column that best describes your progress in each. | ▲ | ▲▲ | ▲▲▲ |
|---|---|---|---|
| distinguish between receipts and payments accounts and income and expenditure accounts | | | |
| prepare receipts and payments accounts | | | |
| prepare accounts for revenue-generating activities, e.g. refreshments, subscriptions | | | |
| prepare income and expenditure accounts and statements of financial position | | | |
| make adjustments to financial statements as detailed in Unit 5.1 (sole traders) | | | |
| define and calculate the accumulated fund. | | | |

## Support

1   Identify six forms of income for a club or society.

2   List the financial statements that may be produced by a club or society.

3   Describe the key differences between the accounting records of profit-making and non-profit making organisations.

4   Ylber craft club was founded in 1977 to provide crafting and social facilities to its members. The club has a café that provides refreshments and a shop that sells a range of craft materials and supplies. On 1 March 2017, the club had $10 500 in the bank account. For the year ended 28 February 2018, the treasurer provided the following list of receipts and payments.

| | $ |
|---|---|
| Subscriptions received | 10 000 |
| Revenue from sales of craft materials and supplies | 6 000 |
| Café revenue | 8 900 |
| Purchases of craft materials for resale | 2 000 |
| Wages – knitting coach | 1 500 |
| Wages – sales assistant | 3 500 |
| Wages – café staff | 2 750 |
| Rent and rates | 2 900 |
| Heat and light | 1 000 |
| General expenses | 300 |
| Purchase of craft equipment | 2 000 |
| National knitting and sewing competition: entrance fees received | 3 500 |
| National knitting and sewing competition: cost of prizes | 750 |

All of the receipts were paid into the bank account and all payments were made by cheque.

Prepare the receipts and payments account of Ylber craft club for the year ended 28 February 2018.

5  Highlands steam railway society has provided the following information relating to its subscriptions for the year ended 31 March 2018.

| | Balances as at 1 April 2017 | Balances as at 31 March 2018 |
|---|---|---|
| | $ | $ |
| Subscriptions in arrears | 350 | 320 |
| Subscriptions paid in advance | 330 | 370 |

During the year, the railway society received $3522 in respect of subscriptions.

Prepare a subscriptions account for the Highlands steam railway society for the year ended 31 March 2018.

6  Bali football society has provided the following information relating to its subscriptions for the year ended 30 April 2018.

| | Balances as at 1 May 2017 | Balances as at 30 April 2018 |
|---|---|---|
| | $ | $ |
| Subscriptions in arrears | 1120 | 1250 |
| Subscriptions paid in advance | 1350 | 1500 |

During the year, the Bali football society received $13 595 in respect of subscriptions.

The society has been informed that $1100 owing at 1 May 2017 will not be recovered. The amount is to be treated as an irrecoverable debt.

Prepare a subscriptions account for the Bali football society for the year ended 30 April 2018.

7  Sweet Treats baking club operates a café for its members. Prepare an income statement for the café for the year ended 31 July 2018 based on the following information.

| | $ |
|---|---|
| Café takings | 33 865 |
| Payments to café suppliers | 11 563 |
| Café wages | 11 100 |

| | Balances as at 1 August 2017 | Balances as at 31 July 2018 |
|---|---|---|
| | $ | $ |
| Café trade payables | 1352 | 1277 |
| Café inventories | 1190 | 197 |

## Practice

8  The following are the details relating to Blue Harbour Tennis Club – which is a club run for children in the local community. The financial details available for 2018 are as follows:

| | 1 January 2018 | 31 December 2018 |
|---|---|---|
| | $ | $ |
| Subscriptions owing | 800 | 1300 |
| Subscriptions paid in advance | 250 | 480 |
| Cash at bank | 1400 | 2400 (overdrawn) |
| Rent of clubhouse accrued | 720 | 1080 |
| Equipment | 10000 | 10400 |
| Snack bar inventory | 260 | 160 |
| Payables for snack bar purchases | 120 | 90 |

During 2018 the following payments were recorded.

| | $ |
|---|---|
| Snack bar purchases | 920 |
| Rent of clubhouse and pitch | 4600 |
| New equipment | 1000 |
| Heating and lighting | 500 |
| Telephone | 230 |
| Transport costs | 500 |
| Hire of equipment for events | 378 |
| Costs of running events | 222 |
| Stationery | 150 |

The following revenues were also received over the same period.

| | $ |
|---|---|
| Subscriptions | 1300 |
| Income from events | 2460 |
| Snack bar sales | 940 |

Prepare for the club:

**(a)** The subscriptions account for 2018

**(b)** An income and expenditure account for the year ended 31 December 2018

**(c)** A statement of affairs as at 1 January 2018

**(d)** A statement of financial position as at 31 December 2018.

## Stretch

9  Discuss the double entry book-keeping principles applied in a receipts and payments account.

10 Describe how the matching principle is applied when producing a subscriptions account for a club or society.

11 When accounting for a life membership scheme in a club, how would you decide on how much of the life membership income to include each year in the income and expenditure account?

12 How would you treat subscriptions that were owing for more than one year in the accounts of a club?

## Unit review

1  Which of the following will appear in an income and expenditure account?

   **(a)** Accrued expenses

   **(b)** Bank balance

   **(c)** Depreciation

   A  (a) and (b)        B  (a) and (c)        C  (b) and (c)        D  (a), (b) and (c)

**2** Which of the following will appear as current assets in a statement of financial position for a club or society?

   **A** Subscriptions due and unpaid       **C** Subscriptions paid in advance

   **B** Subscriptions irrecoverable          **D** Subscriptions received

**3** Which of the following is the equivalent of a cash book for a club or society?

   **A** Accumulated fund account         **C** Receipts and payments account

   **B** Income and expenditure account    **D** Statement of financial position

**4** Which of the following is the equivalent of capital for a club or society?

   **A** Accumulated fund              **C** Equity invested

   **B** Deficit                       **D** Surplus

# 5.5 Manufacturing accounts

## Check your progress

Read the unit objectives below. Tick the column that best describes your progress in each.

| | | | |
|---|---|---|---|
| distinguish between direct and indirect costs | | | |
| understand direct materials, direct labour, prime cost and factory overheads | | | |
| understand and make adjustments for work in progress | | | |
| calculate factory cost of production | | | |
| prepare manufacturing accounts: income statements and statements of financial position | | | |
| make adjustments to financial statements as detailed in Unit 5.1 (sole traders). | | | |

## Support

1   Decide whether the following costs belong in the prime cost or factory overheads sections of the manufacturing account, or in the income statement:

Depreciation of equipment, Factory rent, Wages of factory manager, Purchases of raw materials, Carriage outwards, Depreciation of office equipment, Office rent, Direct wages, Royalties

2   Calculate the cost of raw materials consumed from the following information.

| | $ |
|---|---|
| Inventory of raw materials as at 1 April 2017 | 5670 |
| Inventory of raw materials as at 31 March 2018 | 6910 |
| Purchases of raw materials | 45655 |
| Carriage inwards on raw materials | 290 |
| Purchases returns | 1125 |

3   From the following information prepare the prime cost calculation for the manufacturing account for the year ended 31 May 2018.

| | $ |
|---|---|
| Inventory of raw materials as at 1 June 2017 | 8070 |
| Inventory of raw materials as at 31 May 2018 | 7986 |
| Purchases of raw materials | 99405 |
| Direct wages | 87560 |
| Royalties | 2311 |

## Practice

**4** Identify and discuss two limitations of preparing a manufacturing account.

**5** Why do some businesses transfer finished goods to the trading account at more than cost price?

**6** Arboleda manufacturers has provided the following details of its factory costs for the year ended 30 November 2018.

| | $ |
|---|---|
| Opening inventory of raw materials | 12000 |
| Raw materials purchased | 124000 |
| Direct wages | 148000 |
| Royalties paid | 1600 |
| Depreciation of factory equipment | 11000 |
| Factory rent | 11700 |
| General indirect expenses | 11100 |
| Closing inventory of raw materials | 12600 |
| Work in progress: 1 December 2017 | 18000 |
| 30 November 2018 | 12000 |

Prepare the manufacturing account for Arboleda manufacturers for the year ended 30 November 2018. Clearly show the prime cost and manufacturing cost of goods completed.

**7** The following data relates to the year ended 31 December 2018.

| | $ |
|---|---|
| Inventory of raw materials as at 1 January 2018 | 29670 |
| Inventory of work in progress as at 1 January 2018 | 37020 |
| Purchases of raw materials | 235500 |
| Carriage inwards on raw materials | 369 |
| Purchases returns | 3369 |
| Direct wages | 203025 |
| Royalties | 5250 |
| Indirect wages | 118500 |
| Rent | 22950 |
| Factory running costs | 16470 |
| Equipment at cost | 56700 |
| Provision for depreciation in equipment | 15600 |

**Additional information:**

- As at 31 December 2018 inventory was valued at:
  Raw materials $23529
  Work in progress $42669
- 75% of the rent is apportioned to the factory overheads, the remainder is apportioned to the income statement.
- Rent accrued totalled $1170
- Running costs prepaid totalled $570
- Equipment is depreciated using the reducing balance method at 20%.

Prepare a manufacturing account for the year ended 31 December 2018.

## Stretch

8   The following data relates to the year ended 31 December 2018.

**Additional information:**

- Inventory was valued at 31 December 2018 as follows:

    Raw materials $31 308

    Work in progress $33 088

    Finished goods $68 820

- Depreciation is provided as follows:

    Factory machinery: Reducing balance method at 25%

    Factory property: Straight line method with a useful life of 50 years and no residual value.

- Rent is divided equally between factory overheads and the income statement and $1580 had been prepaid in advance of 2019.

- Heating expenses are allocation between factory overheads and the income statement in a 2 : 1 ratio, with $432 accrued.

- Office administration costs accrued at the year end total $10 900.

| | $ | $ |
|---|---|---|
| Sales | | 1 134 000 |
| Inventory as at 1 January 2018: | | |
| Raw materials | 28 480 | |
| Work in progress | 34 662 | |
| Finished goods | 57 956 | |
| Direct wages | 290 600 | |
| Office administration | 87 000 | |
| Indirect wages | 177 136 | |
| Heating expenses | 13 572 | |
| Royalties | 8 468 | |
| Factory maintenance | 23 780 | |
| Purchases returns | | 2 426 |
| Purchases of raw materials | 270 000 | |
| Distribution costs | 15 300 | |
| Rent | 29 048 | |
| Factory machinery | 175 200 | |
| Factory property | 500 000 | |
| Provision for depreciation: | | |
| Factory machinery | | 10 870 |

Prepare a manufacturing account for the year ended 31 December 2018.

## Unit review

1   Which of the following are used when calculating cost of production?

**(a)** Inventory of finished goods

**(b)** Inventory of raw materials

**(c)** Closing work in progress

**(d)** Opening work in progress

A   (a), (b) and (c)

B   (a), (b) and (d)

C   (b), (c) and (d)

D   (a), (b), (c) and (d)

2   What is calculated as direct materials + direct labour + direct expenses?

A   Gross profit

B   Prime cost

C   Production cost

D   Profit for the year

3   Which of the following are current assets in a manufacturing company's statement of financial position?

**(a)**  Closing work in progress

**(b)**  Closing inventory of finished goods

**(c)**  Money owed by a customer

**(d)**  Money owed to a supplier

A   (a), (b) and (c)     B   (a), (b) and (d)     C   (a), (c) and (d)     D   (b), (c) and (d)

# 5.6 Incomplete records

## Check your progress

| Read the unit objectives below. Tick the column that best describes your progress in each. | ▲ | ▲▲ | ▲▲▲ |
|---|---|---|---|
| explain the disadvantages of not maintaining a full set of accounting records | | | |
| prepare opening and closing statements of affairs | | | |
| calculate profit for the year from changes in capital over time | | | |
| calculate sales, purchases, gross profit, trade receivables, trade payables and other figures from incomplete information | | | |
| prepare income statements and statements of financial position from incomplete records | | | |
| make adjustments to financial statements as detailed in Unit 5.1 (sole traders) | | | |
| apply the techniques of mark-up, margin and inventory turnover to arrive at missing figures. | | | |

## Support

1 Explain how a statement of affairs is used in completing records.

2 Describe how to calculate profit from changes in a business's capital.

3 Marc has not maintained accounting records so his accountant has not been able to prepare an accurate set of financial statements. Marc has been able to establish the following details.

| 1 March 2017 | Assets | $157080 | Liabilities | $14200 |
|---|---|---|---|---|
| 28 February 2018 | Assets | $167400 | Liabilities | $16980 |

During the financial year, Marc withdrew $129000 for personal use. He did not introduce any further capital into the business.

Calculate:

**(a)** the opening and closing capital for Marc business

**(b)** the business's profit for the year.

4 A retailer can supply the info below relating to past trading for the year ended 31 March 2018. Prepare the income statement for the year ended 31 March 2018.

| Mark-up | 25% |
|---|---|
| Purchases | $154000 |
| Opening inventory | $14890 |
| Closing inventory | $15210 |

5 A sole trader has provided the following information.

| | As at 1 July 2017 | As at 30 June 2018 |
|---|---|---|
| Trade receivables | $147600 | $153600 |
| Trade payables | $139400 | $140400 |

| Receipts from trade receivables | 1663200 | Payments to trade payables | 1498800 |
| Cash sales | 124000 | Cash purchases | 315300 |

Calculate the total sales and total purchases.

6 Theba operates as a sole trader. She has full bank account details but has not maintained full accounting records. As at 1 July 2017, her bank balance was $25400. She has provided the following details for receipts and payments.

| Receipts | $ | Payments | $ |
|---|---|---|---|
| Receipts from trade receivables | 1663200 | Payments to trade payables | 1498800 |
| Cash sales | 124000 | Administration expenses | 139240 |
| | | Drawings | 176800 |
| | | Salaries | 180000 |
| | | Heat and light | 17600 |
| | | Insurance | 13800 |
| | | Equipment | 116000 |

Calculate Theba's bank balance as at June 2018.

## Practice

7 Afaaq is running his own computer software design business. He has not kept full financial records for the year but has provided the following information.

| Statement of affairs | | |
|---|---|---|
| | As at 1 January 2018 | As at 31 December 2018 |
| | $ | $ |
| Fixtures and fittings | 5600 | 7476 |
| Computer equipment | 2240 | 2890 |
| Trade payables | 432 | 877 |
| Trade receivables | 1414 | 1313 |
| Bank balance | 875 | (890) |
| Loan (10 years) | 5000 | 5000 |

In addition, Afaaq bought a car for private use during the year using cash takings worth $5600. He also took $2200 cash each month out of the business for personal use. Calculate Afaaq's profit for 2018.

- He bought a car for private use using cash takings worth $5600
- He took $2200 cash each month out of the business for personal use.

Calculate Afaaq's profit for 2018.

8 A golf club sells golfing shoes to members at a subsidised rate to raise cash for the club. There was a break-in on the night of 18 July 2018. The following information is available.

| | |
|---|---|
| Inventory of golfing shoes as at 1 July 2018 (at cost value) | $130 |
| Inventory of golfing shoes as at 31 July 2018 (at cost value) | $30 |
| Purchases of golfing shoes during July 2018 | $980 |
| Sale of golfing shoes during July 2018 | $1000 |

The club sells the shoes at a mark-up of one-third on top of cost.

Calculate the cost of the golfing shoes that were stolen on 18 July 2018.

## Stretch

9  Atsuko operates as a sole trader but has not kept full records. She has supplied the following information.

| Receipts and payments account for 2018 | | | | |
|---|---|---|---|---|
| | $ | | | $ |
| Balance b/d | 4890 | Payments to payables | | 62455 |
| Receipts from receivables | 75680 | General expenses | | 7131 |
| Cash sales | 32100 | Rent | | 1780 |
| | | Equipment | | 6600 |
| | | Balance c/d | | 34704 |
| | 112670 | | | 112670 |

| Assets and liabilities | | |
|---|---|---|
| | 1 January 2018 | 31 December 2018 |
| | $ | $ |
| Premises | 140000 | 140000 |
| Equipment | 24000 | 21700 |
| Motor cars | 12500 | 9700 |
| Trade payables | 4802 | 6660 |
| Trade receivables | 8708 | 11901 |
| General expenses owing | 231 | 555 |
| Inventory | 4890 | 6122 |
| Rent prepaid | 66 | 110 |

In addition, all the cash sales were banked after she took personal drawings of $120 per week.

Prepare the income statement and the statement of financial position for Atsuko as at 31 December 2018.

## Unit review

1  Which of the following ratios has 'cost of sales' included in the formula?

A  Gross margin

B  Rate of inventory turnover

C  Trade payables turnover

D  Trade receivables turnover

2  Boris started operating as a sole trader with capital of $200000. He took a 10-year loan of $75000 to buy equipment for his organisation. Calculate Boris's capital employed.

A  $75000          B  $125000          C  $200000          D  $275000

3  A business has a mark-up of 25%. What is its gross margin percentage?

A  10%          B  20%          C  25%          D  30%

# Chapter 5 review

1 Which of the following accounting statements is represented by capital = assets – liabilities?

   A Appropriation account
   B Income statement

   C Statement of changes in equity
   D Statement of financial position

2 Which of the following is a non-current liability?

   A Debenture
   B Loan repayable within one year

   C Overdraft
   D Trade payable

3 In which section of a statement of financial position would 'accumulated depreciation' appear?

   A Current assets
   B Current liabilities

   C Non-current assets
   D Non-current liabilities

4 Which of the following appears in a limited company's statement of financial position?

   **(a)** Closing equity
   **(b)** Drawings

   **(c)** General reserves
   **(d)** Interim dividends

   A (a), (b) and (c)      B (a), (c) and (d)      C (b), (c) and (d)      D (a), (b), (c) and (d)

5 Which of the following calculates cost of sales?

   A Opening inventory + purchases – closing inventory
   B Opening inventory – purchases – closing inventory
   C Opening inventory + purchases + closing inventory
   D Opening inventory – purchases + closing inventory

6 Which of the following are current liabilities in a statement of financial position?

   **(a)** Bank overdraft
   **(b)** Drawings

   **(c)** Money owed to a supplier
   **(d)** Trade payables

   A (a), (b) and (c)      B (a), (c) and (d)      C (b), (c) and (d)      D (a), (b), (c) and (d)

7 In which of the following partnership accounting records would interest on drawings appear?

   A Fixed capital account
   C Partner's current account

   B Income statement
   D Statement of financial position

8 Which of the following appear in the statement of changes in equity?

   **(a)** Administration expenses
   **(c)** Non-current assets

   **(b)** Corporation tax
   **(d)** Retained earnings

   A (a), (b) and (c)      B (a), (c) and (d)      C (a), (b) and (d)      D (b), (c) and (d)

9 In which section of an income statement would 'an item of revenue expenditure' appear?

   A Additional income
   B Cost of sales

   C Expenses
   D Revenue

10 Which of the following are tangible current assets?

   **(a)** Cash at bank
   **(b)** Closing inventory
   A (a), (b) and (c)
   B (a), (b) and (d)

   **(c)** General reserve
   **(d)** Trade receivables
   C (b), (c) and (d)
   D (a), (b), (c) and (d)

**11** Ji-min and Alejo are in partnership selling shop fixtures and fittings.

**(a)** Complete the following table by placing a tick (✓) in the appropriate column to show where each of the items would appear in Ji-min and Alejo's financial statements. The first one has been done for you. **[8]**

| | Item | Trading account | Income statement | Appropriation account | Statement of financial position |
|---|---|---|---|---|---|
| **(i)** | Interest on capital | | | ✓ | |
| **(ii)** | Premises | | | | |
| **(iii)** | Revenue | | | | |
| **(iv)** | Opening inventory | | | | |
| **(v)** | Trade receivables | | | | |
| **(vi)** | Interest on drawings | | | | |
| **(vii)** | Residual profit | | | | |
| **(viii)** | Commission received | | | | |
| **(ix)** | Carriage outwards | | | | |

Ji-min and Alejo prepared the following appropriation account for the year ended 31 December 2018.

| Ji-min and Alejo Appropriation account for the year ended 31 December 2018 | $ | $ | $ |
|---|---|---|---|
| Profit for the year | | | 39 000 |
| | | | |
| Add charge for interest on drawings: | | | |
| Ji-min | | 500 | |
| Alejo | | 500 | |
| | | | 1 000 |
| | | | 40 000 |
| Less salary: Alejo | | 8 000 | |
| | | | |
| Less interest on capital: | | | |
| Ji-min | 3 000 | | |
| Alejo | 4 000 | | |
| | | 7 000 | |
| | | | 15 000 |
| | | | 25 000 |
| Balance of profits shared: | | | |
| Ji-min | | 10 000 | |
| Alejo | | 15 000 | |
| | | | 25 000 |

On 1 January 2017:

- Ji-min had a credit balance of $3000 on her current account.
- Alejo had a debit balance of $1500 on his current account.
- Ji-min and Alejo each withdrew $2000 during the year for their personal use.

**(b)** Prepare the current account for Ji-min and Alejo as at 1 January 2019. [7]

**(c)** Explain why interest on capital is allowed and interest on drawings is charged in a partnership. [5]

[Total 20]

12  An income statement was produced and the following entries remain on the trial balance of Pietrek at the close of business on 31 December 2018.

| | $ | $ |
|---|---|---|
| Machinery | 186000 | |
| Fixtures | 54000 | |
| Provision for depreciation: Machinery | | 28500 |
| Provision for depreciation: Fixtures | | 15600 |
| Provision for bad debts | | 840 |
| Trade receivables | 30600 | |
| Trade payables | | 23400 |
| Bank | 25500 | |
| Capital | | 216000 |
| Drawings | 63000 | |

**Additional information**

- Inventory as at 31 December 2018 was valued at $57366.
- Wages and salaries accrued at 31 December 2018 amounted to $16305.
- General expenses owing at 31 December 2018 were $936.
- Heating expenses paid in 2018 for 2019 amounted to $2295.
- The provision for doubtful debts is to be kept at 5% of trade receivables at the year-end.
- Depreciation is to be provided as follows:

   Machinery: straight-line method (assuming a lifespan of 5 years and no scrap value)

   Fixtures: 20% using reducing balance method.

Operating profit, which was calculated based on the full trial balance and after all the additional information above has been accounted for, was $71 610.

**(a)** Calculate the amounts that were included in the income statement for the year ended 31 December 2018 for the following:

   **(i)**   Depreciation for machinery [1]

   **(ii)**  Depreciation for fixtures [2]

   **(iii)** Provision for doubtful debts [2]

**(b)** Prepare a statement of financial position for Pietrek as at 31 December 2018. [15]

[Total 20]

13  FFG Ltd has an authorised share capital of 600000 $1 ordinary shares and 500000 $1 4% preference share capital. It has issued 80% of its authorised ordinary share capital and 50% of its preference share capital.

The following information is available:

- Operating profit for 2018                          $62400
- General reserve as at 1 January 2018               $17650

The directors have decided to transfer $3000 to the general reserve and pay an ordinary dividend of $0.03 per share.

(a)  Calculate the value of the total dividend for 2018.                                      [4]

(b)  Prepare an extract from the balance sheet for FFG Ltd showing the capital and reserves as at 31 December 2018.                                                                          [8]

(c)  During 2019, the directors plan to issue the remaining ordinary share capital and remaining preference share capital. Prepare the journal entries that would record this share issue – assuming the issue is fully subscribed but money not received until a later date. Narratives are not required.                                                                          [4]

(d)  Two directors disagree with the planned share issue and would prefer to raise finance through a debenture issue. Explain two reasons why raising finance using debentures may be a good idea.                                                                          [4]

[Total 20]

14  The treasurer of the Grenhill Board Games Club has prepared the following receipts and payments account.

| Receipts and payments account for the year ended 31 December 2018 | | | |
|---|---|---|---|
| Receipts | $ | Payments | $ |
| Balance b/d | 900 | Raffle prizes | 68 |
| Membership subscriptions | 1780 | Electricity | 460 |
| Raffle ticket sales | 138 | Rent | 1980 |
| Snack bar sales | 1530 | Payments to bar payables | 774 |
| | | Balance c/d | 1066 |
| | 4348 | | 4348 |

Other information is as follows:

| | 1 Jan 2018 | 31 Dec 2018 |
|---|---|---|
| | $ | $ |
| Equipment | 24000 | 23500 |
| Subscriptions in advance | 44 | 18 |
| Subscriptions owing | 23 | 88 |
| Payables for snack bar inventory | 111 | 99 |
| Electricity owing | 67 | 223 |
| Snack bar inventory | 98 | 214 |

(a)  Prepare a subscriptions account.                                                          [4]

(b)  Prepare an account showing the profit or loss on the club's snack bar.                     [7]

(c)  Prepare an income and expenditure account for the year ended 31 December 2018.             [9]

[Total 20]

15  The following information relates to Bertels Ltd, a small manufacturing business, for the year ended 31 December 2018.

| | $ |
|---|---|
| Purchases of raw materials | 52454 |
| Opening inventory: | |
| Raw materials | 3241 |
| Work in progress | 6574 |
| Finished goods | 11411 |
| Sales returns | 231 |
| Purchases returns | 114 |
| Manufacturing royalties | 556 |
| Direct labour | 48990 |
| Sales | 148000 |
| Factory rent | 8800 |
| Factory heating costs | 2141 |

Additional information as at 31 December 2018:

1  Closing inventory:                    $
   Raw materials                      4556
   Work in progress                  5558
   Finished goods                   14550
2  Accrued direct labour             1890
3  Prepaid factory rent               770

(a) Prepare a manufacturing account for the year ended 31 December 2018.                    [13]

(b) Prepare an extract from the income statement showing clearly the gross profit earned for the year ended 31 December 2018.                    [6]

(c) State where on the balance sheet the prepaid factory rent appears.                    [1]

[Total 20]

16 Kareem is a retailer who does not keep complete records of accounts. He has provided the following information.

| | 31 Dec 2017 | 31 Dec 2018 |
|---|---|---|
| | $ | $ |
| Trade payables | 8771 | 9101 |
| Trade receivables | 14180 | 12767 |
| Inventory | 9990 | 10443 |

A summary of his bank account for the year ended 31 December 2018 is as follows:

| Receipts | $ | Payments | $ |
|---|---|---|---|
| Balance b/d | 4445 | Payments to trade payables | 54890 |
| Receipts from trade receivables | 29900 | Expenses | 14390 |
| Cash sales | 41414 | Insurance | 2313 |
| | | Balance c/d | 4166 |
| | | | |
| | 75759 | | 75759 |

Before banking his cash sales, Kareem takes $180 each week for personal drawings.

(a) Produce a trading account for the year ended 31 December 2018.                    [12]

Kareem has also supplied the following information for the year ended 31 December 2017.

* All sales were cash sales and cash sales banked were $135640 – with the same arrangement for personal drawings as in 2018.
* In addition, he used $5000 of the cash sales receipts to pay for a personal holiday – which was paid before the receipts were banked.
* Sales are based on a mark-up on cost of sales of 25%.
* Inventory as at 1 January 2017 was valued at $7960.

(b) Produce a trading account for the year ended 31 December 2017.                    [8]

[Total 20]

17 Seo-yun, a retail trader, provided the following trial balance as at 31 December 2017.

| | $ | $ |
|---|---|---|
| Capital | | 200000 |
| Loan | | 60000 |
| Drawings | 20000 | |
| Purchases | 250000 | |
| Purchases returns | | 34850 |
| Revenue | | 260000 |
| Sales returns | 8000 | |
| Discounts allowed | 3500 | |
| Discounts received | | 2000 |
| Carriage outwards | 3000 | |
| Carriage inwards | 5000 | |
| Rent received | | 6000 |
| Provision for doubtful debts | | 650 |
| Sundry expenses | 24000 | |
| Wages and salaries | 35000 | |
| Insurance | 24000 | |
| Loan interest | 4000 | |
| Trade receivables | 35000 | |
| Trade payables | | 30000 |
| Cash at bank | | 8000 |
| Inventory as at 1 January 2017 | 20000 | |
| Land and buildings | 90000 | |
| Fixtures and fittings | 30000 | |
| Motor vehicles | 50000 | |
| | 601500 | 601500 |

The following information is also available.

The closing inventory as at 31 December 2017 was valued at $41000.

- $450 owing for a trade receivable should be written off as an irrecoverable debt.
- The provision for doubtful debts is to be adjusted to 2% of the remaining trade receivables.
- Included in the sundry expenses are fixtures and fittings purchased during the year for $8000. This item has not yet been included in the fixtures and fittings account.
- During the year Seo-yun withdrew goods for her personal use, cost $15000. This has not been recorded in the accounts.
- Two-thirds of the loan is repayable this year and the remainder is due to be repaid in 2020.
- No depreciation is charged on non-current assets.

(a) Prepare Seo-yun's income statement as at 31 December 2017. [16]

(b) Discuss two reasons why Seo-yun should change her policy and depreciate her non-current assets. [4]

[Total 20]

# 6 Analysis and interpretation

## 6.1 Calculation and understanding of ratios

### Check your progress

| Read the unit objectives below. Tick the column that best describes your progress in each. | | | |
|---|---|---|---|
| calculate and explain the importance of the following ratios: | | | |
| gross margin | | | |
| profit margin | | | |
| return on capital employed (ROCE) | | | |
| current ratio | | | |
| liquid (acid test) ratio | | | |
| rate of inventory turnover (times) | | | |
| trade receivables turnover (days) | | | |
| trade payables turnover (days). | | | |

### Support

1   Identify two:

   **(a)** profitability ratios

   **(b)** activity or efficiency ratios

   **(c)** liquidity or solvency ratios.

### Practice

2   Sabbir and Co book store has extracted the following information from the financial accounts for the year ended 31 August 2018.

| | $ |
|---|---|
| Revenue | 174 600 |
| Opening inventory | 6 350 |
| Purchases | 89 150 |
| Closing inventory | 8 200 |
| General expenses | 69 840 |
| Drawings | 6 984 |
| Current assets | 24 600 |
| Current liabilities | 16 400 |

Calculate the following ratios.

   **(a)** Current ratio        **(b)** Liquid (acid test) ratio        **(c)** Rate of inventory turnover

**3** Ceri's statement of financial position showed the following assets and liabilities.

| | $ |
| --- | --- |
| Non-current assets | 180000 |
| Current assets | 24000 |
| Current liabilities | 12000 |
| Long-term loan | 72000 |
| Closing inventory | 7000 |

For Ceri's business, calculate:

**(a)** the current ratio

**(b)** the liquid (acid test) ratio (to 2 decimal places).

**4** The following information has been provided for three small retail stores.

| | Store 1 | Store 2 | Store 3 |
| --- | --- | --- | --- |
| | $ | $ | $ |
| Trade receivables | 130000 | 250000 | 150000 |
| Trade payables | 50000 | 75000 | 100000 |
| Credit sales | 235000 | 260000 | 255000 |
| Cash sales | 1000 | 8000 | 2500 |
| Credit purchases | 155000 | 125000 | 135000 |

Calculate the following ratios for each of the three stores (to 2 decimal places).

**(a)** Trade receivables turnover

**(b)** Trade payables turnover

**5** The following information has been provided for three local cafés.

| | Café 1 | Café 2 | Café 3 |
| --- | --- | --- | --- |
| | $ | $ | $ |
| Revenue | 260000 | 500000 | 300000 |
| Gross profit | 100000 | 150000 | 200000 |
| Profit for the year | 70000 | 120000 | 110000 |
| Capital employed | 110000 | 250000 | 70000 |

Calculate the following ratios for each of the three cafés (to 2 decimal places).

**(a)** Gross margin

**(b)** Profit margin

**(c)** Return on capital employed (ROCE)

## Stretch

**6** Discuss how a sole trader's annual financial statements may allow the owner to assess the liquidity of the business.

**7** The following financial data has been provided for three small gyms.

| | Gym 1 | Gym 2 | Gym 3 |
|---|---|---|---|
| | $ | $ | $ |
| Working capital | 75000 | 240000 | 180000 |
| Average inventory for the year | 25000 | 77500 | 92500 |
| Opening inventory | 20000 | 65000 | 35000 |
| Total current liabilities | 75000 | 150000 | 750000 |

Calculate the following ratios for each of the three gyms.

**(a)** Current ratio

**(b)** Liquid (acid test) ratio

**8** M3 Limited is an engineering company. The company has a capital employed of $100000. For the year ended 30 April 2018, it generated revenue of $120000 and a gross margin of 50%. Expenses for the year ended 30 April 2018 totalled $30000.

Calculate M3's:

**(a)** profit margin

**(b)** return on capital employed (ROCE).

## Unit review

**1** Afzal and Michael work in partnership together and are reviewing the profitability of their business. Which ratio would be of interest to Afzal and Michael in this review?

**A** Gross margin

**B** Rate of inventory turnover

**C** Trade payables turnover

**D** Trade receivables turnover

**2** Kateryna operates as a sole trader. At the year end, she has current assets of $100000, current liabilities of $50000 and closing inventory of $25000.

Calculate Kateryna's liquid (acid test) ratio.

**A** 1 : 1      **B** 1.5 : 1      **C** 2 : 1      **D** 2.5 : 1

**3** Tamara purchases goods on credit from Jonatan. Which of Tamara's accounting ratios would Jonatan be interested in?

**A** Gross margin

**B** Rate of inventory turnover

**C** Trade payables turnover

**D** Trade receivables turnover

**4** Adnan provided the following extract from his statement of financial position.

| | $ |
|---|---|
| Non-current assets | 180000 |
| Current assets | 24000 |
| Current liabilities | 12000 |
| Long-term loan | 72000 |

Calculate Adnan's current ratio.

**A** 0.5 : 1      **B** 2.0 : 1      **C** 2.4 : 1      **D** 2.5 : 1

# 6.2 Interpretation of accounting ratios

## Check your progress

| Read the unit objectives below. Tick the column that best describes your progress in each. | ▲ | ▲▲ | ▲▲▲ |
|---|---|---|---|
| prepare and comment on simple statements showing comparison of results for different years | | | |
| make recommendations and suggestions for improving profitability and working capital | | | |
| understand the significance of the difference between the gross margin and the profit margin as an indicator of a business's efficiency | | | |
| explain the relationship of gross profit and profit for the year to the valuation of inventory, rate of inventory turnover, revenue, expenses, and equity. | | | |

## Support

1   Describe what each of the following ratios shows.

   (a) Gross margin                         (e) Trade receivables turnover (days)
   (b) Profit margin                        (f) Trade payables turnover (days)
   (c) Return on capital employed (ROCE)    (g) Current ratio
   (d) Rate of inventory turnover (times)   (h) Liquid (acid test) ratio

2   Identify three negative effects of delaying payment to a trade payable.

## Practice

3   The following data relates to a retailer of bathroom supplies. Calculate relevant activity ratios and comment on your findings.

|  | 2017 | 2018 |
|---|---|---|
|  | $ | $ |
| Credit sales | 325 000 | 380 000 |
| Credit purchases | 189 000 | 201 000 |
| Trade receivables | 22 400 | 38 700 |
| Trade payables | 18 700 | 21 900 |

4   Castleland is a fast-food takeaway business. The owner has calculated her rate of inventory turnover the last year as 330 times. The fast-food takeaway industry average is 300 times per year.

   (a) Explain whether Castleland should be satisfied with its rate of inventory turnover.
   (b) Describe how Castleland could improve its rate of inventory turnover.

5   Abhi operates as a sole trader and provides financial advice to individuals. He has provided the following extract from his financial records.

| | 31 March 2017 | 31 March 2018 |
|---|---|---|
| Revenue received | $400000 | $420000 |
| Gross profit | $220000 | $250000 |
| Expenses | $150000 | $180000 |

(a)  For 2017 and 2018, calculate the gross margin and profit margin ratios.

(b)  Discuss whether Abhi should be satisfied with his financial performance.

(c)  Explain how he could improve his profitability.

6   Explain the implication of a shortage of working capital to a business.

## Stretch

7   Aadesh owns a retail clothing business. He has calculated his gross margin as 25%. A local business enterprise group calculated the sector average as 35%. Discuss why it may be difficult for Aadesh to improve his gross margin.

8   Discuss why it is important for a business to consider the difference between its gross margin and profit margin?

9   Wickets cricket store has calculated its current ratio as 1.2 : 1 and its liquid (acid test) ratio as 0.7 : 1. The sector average for the current ratio is 2 : 1 and for the liquid (acid test) ratio is 1 : 1. Discuss why Wickets may not be concerned about the apparent lower liquidity.

## Unit review

1   Lucia and Stainslaw operate as a partnership. They are reviewing how efficient they are at collecting their debts. Which ratio would be of interest to Lucia and Stanislaw in this review?

A  Gross margin                          C  Trade payables turnover

B  Rate of inventory turnover            D  Trade receivables turnover

2   Polina has calculated her current ratio for 2017 as 2.5 : 1 and for 2018 as 3 : 1. Her current liabilities have remained the same in 2017 and 2018. Which of the following could be a reason for the increase in Polina's current ratio?

A  Decrease in trade payables            C  Decrease in trade receivables

B  Increase in trade payables            D  Increase in trade receivables

3   Which of the following ratios would enable a business to assess its liquidity?

A  Current ratio                         C  Trade payables turnover

B  Gross margin                          D  Trade receivables turnover

4   Chambers office supplies' profit margin has increased over the last three years. Which of the following could be a reason for this increase?

A  Decrease in business assets           C  Decrease in business expenses

B  Increase in business assets           D  Increase in business expenses

# 6.3 Inter-firm comparison

## Check your progress

Read the unit objectives below. Tick the column that best describes your progress in each.

| | ▲ | ▲▲ | ▲▲▲ |
|---|---|---|---|
| understand the problems of inter-firm comparison | | | |
| apply accounting ratios to inter-firm comparisons | | | |

## Support

1   Compare the ratios for two small retailers selling audio-visual equipment below. Which business is performing better? Justify your answer.

| | A–Z Sounds | 123 Music |
|---|---|---|
| Gross margin (%) | 34 | 28 |
| Profit margin (%) | 17 | 15 |
| Return on capital employed (%) | 7 | 9 |
| Current ratio | 1.2 : 1 | 1.6 : 1 |
| Liquid (acid test) ratio | 0.9 : 1 | 1.1 : 1 |
| Rate of inventory turnover (times) | 9 | 11 |
| Trade receivables turnover (days) | 32 | 44 |
| Trade payables turnover (days) | 45 | 51 |

## Practice

2   Hill top runners is a retail store which sells sports equipment. It has provided the following ratio data below for its business and for that of its local competitor, Summit hiking supplies. Use inter-firm comparison techniques to advise the management of Hill top runners on how to improve its financial performance.

| | Hill top runners | Summit hiking supplies |
|---|---|---|
| Gross margin | 30% | 45% |
| Profit margin | 25% | 30% |
| Return on capital employed | 21% | 25% |

3   Alain owns ABC manufacturers. He is considering purchasing another manufacturing business, DEF production. He has provided the information below from the financial statements for the two businesses. Advise Alain whether he should purchase DEF production.

| | ABC manufacturers | DEF production |
|---|---|---|
| Closing inventory | $60 000 | $170 000 |
| Cash at bank | $200 000 | $(50 000) |
| Trade receivables | $110 000 | $250 000 |
| Trade payables | $190 000 | $126 000 |

4   The data shown is for two businesses that import clothing to sell in their own country to small clothing shops. Which business do you think is performing better? Justify your answer.

|  | Fashion Supplies Ltd | Quality Clothing Ltd |
|---|---|---|
| Trade receivables days | 22 days | 35 days |
| Trade payables days | 30 days | 36 days |
| Rate of inventory turnover | 12 times | 24 times |

## Stretch

5   Argo plc has provided the ratio information below for Argo plc and Argus plc, its local competitor. Prepare a business report to assess the liquidity of Argo plc to present to the board of directors.

|  | Argo plc | Argus plc |
|---|---|---|
| Gross margin | 59% | 32% |
| Profit margin | 34% | 20% |
| Return on capital employed | 53% | 18% |

## Unit review

1   Bence compares his annual financial statements with those of similar local businesses. Which one of the following will show that Bence is controlling the amount paid for his goods for resale?

A   Cash in hand                     C   Opening inventory

B   Cost of sales                    D   Trade receivables

2   A business wishes to use inter-firm comparison to review its efficiency. Which of the following ratios would allow this comparison to take place?

A   Current ratio                    C   Liquid (acid test) ratio

B   Gross margin                     D   Rate of inventory turnover

3   Which ratio would identify inefficient purchasing when completing an inter-firm comparison?

A   Current ratio                    C   Liquid (acid test) ratio

B   Gross margin                     D   Rate of inventory turnover

4   Simba Ltd has calculated its accounting ratios for the year ended 31 March 2018. Which of the following ratios would Simba Ltd compare with a local competitor in order to review the profitability of its operations?

A   Current ratio                    C   Liquid (acid test) ratio

B   Gross margin                     D   Rate of inventory turnover

# 6.4 Interested parties

## Check your progress

| Read the unit objectives below. Tick the column that best describes your progress in each. | ▲ | ▲▲ | ▲▲▲ |
|---|---|---|---|
| explain the uses of accounting information by the following interested parties for decision making: | | | |
| owners, managers, trade payables, banks, investors, club members | | | |
| other interested parties such as governments and tax authorities. | | | |

## Support

1   Identify five interested parties of a leisure centre.

2   Identify the features in the financial statements of a sports club that would be of interest to its members.

## Practice

3   Discuss why a bank would be interested in the financial statements of a sole trader.

4   Explain the uses of accounting information by the following interested parties for decision-making.

(a) Owners          (c) Trade payables          (e) Local and national government
(b) Managers        (d) Club members

## Stretch

5   Discuss the conflict of interest that may occur between a stakeholder and a shareholder.

6   Analyse the reasons for a potential investor reviewing the financial statements of businesses.

## Unit review

1   Which of the following best defines the term 'company shareholder'?

   A  An individual employed by a business organisation
   B  An individual who owns a business organisation
   C  An individual with an interest in a business organisation
   D  An individual who lends funds to a business organisation

2   Which of the following is an external stakeholder of a business?

   A  Customer          B  Employee          C  Manager          D  Owner

3   Which of the following stakeholders would be **most** interested in the profitability of a business organisation?

   A  Customer          B  Employee          C  Manager          D  Owner

# 6.5 Limitations of accounting statements

## Check your progress

| Read the unit objectives below. Tick the column that best describes your progress in each. | ▲ | ▲▲ | ▲▲ |
|---|---|---|---|
| recognise the limitations of accounting statements due to such factors as: | | | |
| historic cost | | | |
| difficulties of definition | | | |
| non-financial aspects. | | | |

## Support

1  Explain why business location cannot be included in the accounting statements of a business.

## Practice

2  Explain the difference between quantitative information and qualitative information.

3  Identify five types of qualitative information that would assist a business in reviewing its financial performance.

4  Describe two examples of conflicting accounting definitions.

5  Describe, with an example, why historic cost is a limitation to a reader of financial information.

## Stretch

6  Taj produces financial statements at the end of each year for his sole trader business. Explain to Taj the limitation of the financial statements that he prepares each year.

7  Explain how a business should value its premises in the annual financial statements.

8  The following are extracts from the financial statements of a fashion retailer.

|  | 2017 | 2018 |
|---|---|---|
|  | $ | $ |
| Revenue | 48 000 | 47 000 |
| Cost of sales | 27 000 | 19 500 |
| Gross profit | 21 000 | 27 500 |
| Expenses | 8 000 | 14 000 |
| Net profit | 13 000 | 13 500 |

Additional information:

In 2017, 5% of the workforce left the company

In 2018, 16% of the workforce left the company.

In 2017, due to concerns over declining profits, the managers of the business decided to move from paying sales assistants a fixed salary to paying them entirely based on how much they sold. This move was not popular.

**(a)** Did the move to the new method of paying sales assistants improve profitability?

**(b)** Should the managers be pleased with this decision?

## Unit review

1   Which limitation of accounting statements is defined as the recording of financial transactions at original cost price?

    **A** Difficulties in definition          **C** Historic cost

    **B** Financial reporting                **D** Non-financial aspects

2   Which of the following are **not** limitations of accounting statements?

    **(a)** Accounting statements only include financial aspects

    **(b)** All numerical data is estimated

    **(c)** Business organisations can omit transactions

    **(d)** Financial records are incomplete

    **A** (a), (b) and (c)     **B** (a), (c) and (d)     **C** (a), (b), (c) and (d)     **D** (b), (c) and (d)

3   Which of the following accurately calculates the net book value of a motor vehicle?

    **A** Historic cost less annual depreciation

    **B** Historic cost less cumulative depreciation

    **C** Historic cost plus annual depreciation

    **D** Historic cost plus cumulative depreciation

4   Which of the following are financial aspects of a business?

    **(a)** Cost of sales

    **(b)** Goodwill

    **(c)** Working capital

    **A** (a) and (b)     **B** (a) and (c)     **C** (b) and (c)     **D** (a), (b) and (c)

# Chapter 6 review

1   A business provided the following information for the year ended 31 December 2018.

| | $ |
|---|---|
| Sales revenue | 800 000 |
| Cost of sales | 200 000 |
| Expenses | 100 000 |

What is the gross margin?

A  10%                    B  25%                    C  50%                    D  75%

2   How is the return on capital employed calculated for a limited company?

A  Profit after interest × capital employed

B  Profit after interest ÷ capital employed

C  Profit before interest × capital employed

D  Profit before interest ÷ capital employed

3   Which of the following represents capital employed for a limited company?

A  Issued shares + reserves + non-current liabilities

B  Issued shares − reserves − non-current liabilities

C  Issued shares + reserves − non-current liabilities

D  Issued shares − reserves + non-current liabilities

4   Which of the following ratios would be of most interest when considering the solvency of a business?

A  Current ratio                          C  Trade receivables turnover

B  Gross margin                          D  Return on capital employed

5   A business provided the following information as at 31 December 2017.

| | $ |
|---|---|
| Trade receivables | 9 000 |
| Credit sales | 27 000 |
| Cash sales | 18 000 |

What is the trade receivables turnover to the nearest day?

A  73 days                  B  122 days                  C  183 days                  D  365 days

6   Which of the following ratio groups measures a business's efficiency?

A  Current ratio                          Trade receivables turnover

B  Rate of inventory turnover            Liquid (acid test) ratio

C  Liquid (acid test) ratio              Return on capital employed

D  Trade receivables turnover            Rate of inventory turnover

7   A business's gross margin has increased over the past year. Which of the following could explain this increase?

A  Decrease in cost of sales            C  Decrease in expenses

B  Increase in cost of sales            D  Increase in expenses

**8** Which of the following is a measure of a business's ability to pay its short-term debts?

**A** Current ratio            **C** Trade receivables turnover

**B** Gross margin            **D** Return on capital employed

**9** A business provided the following financial information.

| | $ |
|---|---|
| Sales revenue | 150000 |
| Cost of sales | 50000 |
| Opening inventory | 12000 |
| Closing inventory | 18000 |
| Expenses | 25000 |

Calculate the business's profit margin.

**A** 25%            **B** 50%            **C** 75%            **D** 100%

**10** An investor is reviewing a limited company's financial statements. Which of the following will contain information about the company's debentures?

**A** Appropriation account            **C** Statement of changes in equity

**B** Income statement            **D** Statement of financial position

**11** Hua runs a bed and breakfast business, operating as a sole trader.

**(a)** Identify four limitations Hua faces operating as a sole trader.      [4]

**(b)** Identify and explain three limitations of the accounting statements Hua will produce.      [9]

**(c)** Identify three ratios Hua could use to measure the profitability of her business.      [3]

**(d)** As a seasonal business, a bed and breakfast has very few customers in the winter. Explain two possible effects of Hua having insufficient working capital during the winter months.      [4]

           **[Total 20]**

**12** Ludwig runs a music store, operating as a sole trader. He has provided the following financial data for the year ended 31 December 2018.

| Ludwig's music store | |
|---|---|
| | $ |
| For the year ended 31 December 2018: | |
| Revenue | 260000 |
| Gross profit | 100000 |
| Profit for the year | 70000 |
| Capital employed | 110000 |
| | |
| **As at 31 December 2018:** | |
| Inventory | 11000 |
| Trade receivables | 4000 |
| Bank | 3500 |
| Trade payables | 12500 |

**(a)** Calculate the following ratios for Ludwig (to 2 d.p.).

     **(i)** Gross margin      [3]

     **(ii)** Profit margin      [3]

     **(iii)** Return on capital employed (ROCE)      [3]

**(b)** Ludwig is looking to attract a partner to help run the music store. He is worried that his business is not performing as well as similar music stores in his region. A financial adviser reassures Ludwig telling him that Ludwig's music store is performing well.

Relevant information that the financial adviser provides includes:

- Average gross margin for similar music stores in the region: 45%

- Average profit margin for similar music stores in the region: 33%.

Explain, using the ratios relating to music stores in Ludwig's region, **three** reasons why Ludwig's performance ratios are lower than the average for similar businesses. [6]

**(c)** Calculate the current ratio for Ludwig to (2 d.p.). [3]

**(d)** State whether Ludwig should be happy with his liquidity position. Briefly justify your answer. [2]

[Total 20]

13 Nadeem, a sole trader, received an invoice showing a balance owing of $1000, less 2.5% discount for payment before the month end. Nadeem paid the invoice before the end of the month.

**(a)** Calculate how much Nadeem paid. [1]

**(b)** Identify the type of discount Nadeem was offered. [1]

**(c)** Explain one reason why the supplier would offer the discount. [2]

Nadeem provided the following financial information as at 31 October 2018.

| | $ |
|---|---|
| Non-current assets | 180 000 |
| Current assets | 24 000 |
| Current liabilities | 12 000 |
| Non-current liabilities | 72 000 |
| Closing inventory | 12 000 |
| Opening inventory | 8 000 |

**(d)** Calculate Nadeem's:

   **(i)** Current ratio [3]

   **(ii)** Liquid (acid test) ratio. [3]

**(e)** Explain why Nadeem's manager would be interested in the business's financial statements. [6]

**(f)** Explain two possible comparisons an interested party could make to review Nadeem's business. [4]

[Total 20]

# 7 Accounting principles and policies

## 7.1 Accounting principles

### Check your progress

| Read the unit objectives below. Tick the column that best describes your progress in each. | ▲ | ▲▲ | ▲▲▲ |
|---|---|---|---|
| explain and recognise the application of the following accounting principles: | | | |
| matching | | | |
| business entity | | | |
| consistency | | | |
| duality | | | |
| going concern | | | |
| historic cost | | | |
| materiality | | | |
| money measurement | | | |
| prudence | | | |
| realisation. | | | |

### Support

1    A public limited company would like to include the $30 curtains as a non-current asset in its financial statements. Explain whether this is correct.

2    A sole trader has taken cash from his business to pay for a family holiday.

   (a)  Explain how the sole trader should account for this transaction.

   (b)  Identify the accounting principle that is being applied.

3    Describe how expenses and income must be treated in the financial statements in accordance with the matching principle.

4    Identify three items that cannot be included in financial statements due to the money measurement principle.

## Practice

5 Jabar runs a coffee and cake café. He is preparing his end of year financial statements.

(a) He currently depreciates his coffee machines using the straight line method but thinks this means the machines appear on the balance sheet with unrealistic valuations. He wishes to change his method to the reducing balance method.

(b) Jabar normally caters for a festival every January. He has provided the drinks and cakes for this event for the last ten years and a friend has told him that the festival organiser has said that they will use Jabar's café again. Jabar wishes to include this in the sales income for December as its 'almost certain' that the sales will be made.

(c) An electricity bill is due to be paid in December but Jabar plans on delaying payment until January as he thinks he will not need to include it in this year's expenses if he delays payment.

Advise Jabar on correct procedure, identifying any appropriate principles that may affect your decision.

## Stretch

6 Discuss the importance of having accounting principles and policies when preparing financial accounts for international businesses.

7 Which of the statements would be accurate if the duality principle has been applied?

1 A debit balance c/d will occur when the total of the debit entries is less than the total of the credit entries.

2 A credit balance c/d will occur when the total of the debit entries is less than the total of the credit entries.

3 A credit balance c/d will occur when the total of the credit entries is more than the total of the debit entries.

## Unit review

1 A business values its inventory at the 'lower of cost and net realisable value'. Which accounting principle is being applied?

   **A** Business entity      **B** Consistency      **C** Going concern      **D** Prudence

2 At the end of the financial year, a business makes a charge against the profit for insurance purchased, paid for but not yet consumed. Which accounting principle is being applied?

   **A** Accruals      **B** Business entity      **C** Going concern      **D** Prudence

3 When preparing financial statements, accountants need to ensure that a business will continue to operate for the foreseeable future. Which accounting principle is being defined?

   **A** Business entity      **B** Going concern      **C** Matching      **D** Prudence

4 Which accounting principle is being applied when a business produces its trial balance?

   **A** Business entity      **B** Consistency      **C** Duality      **D** Prudence

# 7.2 Accounting policies

## Check your progress

Read the unit objectives below. Tick the column that best describes your progress in each.

| | ▲ | ▲▲ | ▲▲▲ |
|---|---|---|---|
| recognise the influence of international accounting standards and understand the following objectives in selecting accounting policies: | | | |
| comparability | | | |
| relevance | | | |
| reliability | | | |
| understandability. | | | |

## Support

1   Identify five considerations that will ensure financial statements are reliable.

2   Explain why it is important for financial statements to be relevant to the user of the information.

3   Identify two factors that affect the understandability of financial information.

## Practice

4   Discuss the importance of a multinational company using International Accounting Standards.

## Stretch

5   Research the titles of the following International Accounting Standards (IAS).

   **(a)** IAS 1        **(b)** IAS 2        **(c)** IAS 7        **(d)** IAS 16        **(e)** IAS 33        **(f)** IAS 38

   Discuss in pairs why each of the IAS's may be used by a business.

## Unit review

1   Which objective for selecting accounting policies does the following statement define?

   Accounting information that is timely, useful and will make a difference to an interested party when making a decision.

   **A** Comparability        **B** Relevance        **C** Reliability        **D** Understandability

2   Which objective for selecting accounting policies does the following statement define?

   An accounting policy which states that a business's financial information should be presented in a way that an individual with a reasonable knowledge of business and finance, and a willingness to study the information provided, should be able to understand it.

   **A** Comparability        **B** Relevance        **C** Reliability        **D** Understandability

# Chapter 7 review

1  Which accounting principle states that a business transaction always has two effects on a business?

   **A** Consistency         **B** Duality         **C** Matching         **D** Prudence

2  A limited company depreciates fixtures and fittings at 20% per annum. The policy has not changed since the company was founded. Which accounting principle is being applied?

   **A** Consistency         **B** Duality         **C** Matching         **D** Prudence

3  When preparing an income statement, irrecoverable debts are included in the expenses. Which accounting principle is being applied?

   **A** Business entity         **C** Prudence

   **B** Consistency           **D** Money measurement

4  Which of the following defines the historic cost principle?

   **A** Financial accounts contain only items that have a monetary value

   **B** Financial transactions are maintained on a double entry basis

   **C** Non-current assets are valued at cost less depreciation

   **D** Profit for the year is calculated by deducting expenses from gross profit

5  Which accounting principle is applied when accounting for a provision for doubtful debts?

   **A** Matching         **B** Materiality         **C** Prudence         **D** Realisation

6  This principle states that revenue should be recognised when the exchange of goods or services takes place.

   **A** Duality         **B** Matching         **C** Prudence         **D** Realisation

7  A business would like to record its excellent customer satisfaction ratings as an asset in the statement of financial position. Which accounting principle prevents this?

   **A** Business entity         **C** Historic cost

   **B** Going concern         **D** Money measurement

8  Which of the following is an objective in selecting accounting policies?

   **A** Accruals         **B** Consistency         **C** Prudence         **D** Reliability

9  A business purchases fixtures and fittings for cash. The transaction has been recorded in the cash book and in the fixtures and fittings account. Which accounting principle is being applied when completing this transaction?

   **A** Business entity         **C** Matching

   **B** Duality            **D** Money measurement

10  This principle states that a company's financial records are produced from the viewpoint of the company and not the shareholders.

   **A** Business entity         **C** Matching

   **B** Duality            **D** Money measurement

11  Iram is a sole trader. At the financial year end she has provided the following information as at 31 December 2018.

(a) Define the term 'trial balance'. [2]

(b) Identify and explain the principle that is applied when preparing a trial balance. [3]

(c) Identify two uses of a trial balance. [2]

(d) Prepare Iram's trial balance as at 31 December 2018. [7]

(e) Identify and explain three errors that are not revealed by a trial balance. [6]

[Total 20]

| | $ |
|---|---|
| Cash at bank | 6400 |
| Carriage inwards | 1400 |
| Trade payables | 17200 |
| Trade receivables | 29600 |
| Provision for depreciation: motor vehicles | 5600 |
| Drawings | 48000 |
| General expenses | 780 |
| Insurance | 820 |
| Lighting and heating | 1200 |
| Motor vehicles | 35200 |
| Motor expenses | 1720 |
| Office expenses | 560 |
| Rent and rates | 1800 |
| Purchases | 151200 |
| Revenue | 204000 |
| Capital | 179180 |
| Inventory as at 31 December 2017 | 16800 |
| Wages and salaries | 10500 |
| Freehold land | 100000 |

12  Fatima, a sole trader, runs a small clothing store. She operates a double entry book-keeping system.

(a) Identify and explain the accounting principle that Fatima is applying. [2]

(b) Complete the table by stating the accounts which should be debited and credited when entering the transactions into the appropriate double entry accounts. The first one has been done for you. [10]

| | Transaction | Account to be debited | Account to be credited |
|---|---|---|---|
| (i) | Purchase of fixtures and fittings, paying by cheque | Fixtures and fittings | Bank |
| (ii) | Payment of employee wages by cash | | |
| (iii) | Cash sales | | |
| (iv) | Receipt of commission by cheque | | |
| (v) | Fatima withdrew cash from the bank for her own use | | |
| (vi) | Sale of goods on credit to Arjun | | |

Fatima has been informed that the quality of information in her financial statements will be measured in terms of relevance and reliability.

(c) Define:

(i) Reliability [2]

(ii) Relevance [2]

(d) Identify and explain the accounting principle which informs Fatima that her personal finances need to be kept separately from those of the clothing store. [4]

[Total 20]